LEGEND OF THE LOTUS SEVEN

by Dennis Ortenburger

Dedicated to my most avid readers,
Marlene, Kip and Renn

LEGEND OF THE
LOTUS SEVEN

Editor: Sarah Eppenbach
Editorial Consultant: Doug Nye
Graphic Consultant: Paul Pfanner
Design: Rex Irvine Graphics
Typography: Nova Typesetting
Printing: Times Printers Sdn. Bhd.

Osprey ISBN 0-85045-411-5
Newport Press ISBN 0-930880-06-04

Library of Congress card number 81-81134

Printed in Singapore

Produced by The Newport Press, 1001 West 18th St.,
Costa Mesa, California 92627 for the publishers,
Osprey Publishing Ltd, 12-14 Long Acre, London WC2E 9LP,
England, a member company of the George Philip Group.

Distributed in the USA by

Motorbooks International
Publishers & Wholesalers Inc
Osceola, Wisconsin 54020, USA

CONTENTS

Acknowledgements

The truly useful information in this book has come from the many enthusiasts who contributed personal accounts of their experiences with the Lotus Seven. The list of acknowledgments has to begin with Doug Nye, who's written more about Lotus and knows more about their operation than anyone. Thanks also go to my editor, Sarah Eppenbach and my publisher, Rich McCormack, who both wore out more than a few blue pencils on my behalf. And to my wife, Marlene, who translated what's been called a cross between Sanscrit and Chinese into typewritten English.

My thanks go to Tony Caldersmith, former Lotus service manager who designed the Seven's first weather equipment. From his home in Australia, Tony sent recollections about the car's early production as well as the Australian Clubman scene, where the Seven played an important role. Fond regards go to Frank Costin, who shared many vignettes about aerodynamics, as well as his own story of building a "Lotus Seven-beater" for the race track. Also warm thanks to the Lotus fairy Godfather, invisible financial wizard Peter Kirwan-Taylor, who provided invaluable insight into the calamitous days of uncertain future.

Special recognition goes to Richard Bourne of the Historic Lotus Register for supplying details about Lotus chassis numbers unavailable elsewhere. I also thank Adrien Schagen of Sydney, Australia, for loaning me his most extensive literature collection and providing numerous photographs. Tom White of AutomobileMews in San Diego, California, helped us locate cover car owner Don Pisor, and I thank them both for their cooperation

Two long-time friends and Seven racers, Dave Bean and Jim Gallagher, were kind enough to read over the manuscript, as was Graham Nearn of Caterham Cars. Peter Ecury in Holland and Duarte Coelho in Portugal provided extraordinary research assistance. Jon Derisley of the British Racing Drivers Club, David Kaplan of DSK Cars, Inc., Joop Dankervoort, builder of the Netherlands Seven, and SCCA champion Tom Robertson all contributed accounts of construction, design and racing of Lotus Sevens. Another special thanks to Bob Bent, who was right behind me at Laguna Seca in 1977 when he crashed his borrowed Seven (see Chapter 4).

I am indebted to the editors and publishers of *Road & Track* for allowing access to their files and permitting road tests to be reprinted.

Many others who gave no less significant bits and pieces are listed under photo credits or mentioned in the text. All in all, a splendid group of people that brought me to a significant conclusion: only nice guys drive Lotus Sevens.

Preface: Making Friends With A Seven

My fascination for the Lotus Seven is second only to that for the Lotus Elite, and I remember making their acquaintances in the early 1960's when I was in my teens. Both were tremendously appealing, but a greater contrast between two siblings could scarcely be imagined. The Elite played heavily to my burgeoning sense of aesthetics. I was awed by the perfect proportions and elegant lines. Clearly, this was class.

The Seven was something else again: the utterly basic sports car. An enthusiast's car. An affordable car. Not a thoroughbred, but a quarter horse. The Seven wouldn't win any beauty contests, but the driving position, the alloy panels and the side exhaust all spelled *performance*, and that was something every 18-year-old believed in.

The Seven was extraordinarily tempting, but difficulties presented themselves at once. How in the world could I get away with driving that on the street? Assuming the car could be licensed and insured (I had my doubts about the latter, recalling the agent's rather extreme reaction to my relatively innocent inquiry about an MG-TD), every cop from Hollywood to Manhattan Beach would have my picture on his sun visor.

In the end, the Elite proved the more powerful draw and I have nurtured the love affair for some 14 years. I've never been sorry about the choice, but occasionally I find myself wondering what it would be like to roar up the Pacific Coast Highway on a fine afternoon, jammed into the cockpit of my own Super Seven. I guess I'll never know the answer to that question, but I've been fortunate in coming close. By diligently traveling in the right circles over the years, I've managed to sample all of the Sevens, from the Series 1 to the Series 4. Researching this book enabled me to relive the dream again and again.

Normally, the story of a particularly interesting car isn't attempted until some time after production has ceased, but if I'd waited until then to indulge myself, you wouldn't be reading this book. The fact that the Lotus Seven is still being constructed in two countries is a measure of the fanatical devotion enthusiasts have toward the car. Can you imagine? An automobile too good to let die! Well, that's the stuff legends are made of, and the Seven is nothing short of that.

1 Car Fo

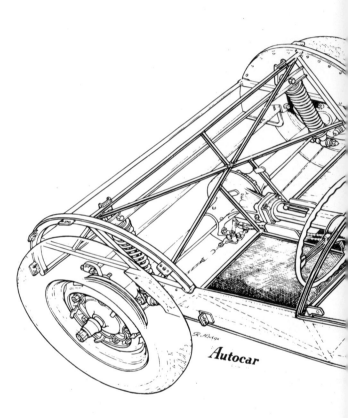

This cutaway drawing of the Lotus
Mark 6 by R.H. Hodge appeared in the
September 25, 1953 issue of
The Autocar. The accompanying story
described this "successful small
sports car available for home
construction" in considerable detail.

Mark 6: "A Sports Home Construction"

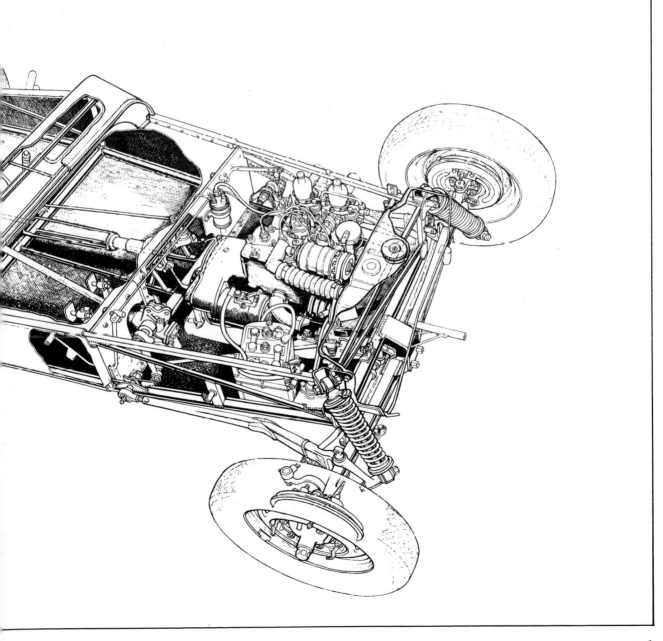

In 1953 the Lotus Engineering Company, Ltd. was hardly more than a garage with a sign above the door at No. 7 Tottenham Lane in North London. Colin Chapman was twenty-five years old and ran the fledgling business as a part-time venture. His profession was engineering and his regular job was with the British Aluminium Company. Chapman had made a modest reputation for himself and his Lotus cars in that feisty English auto sport called "Trials." Even more success came in club level circuit racing with Austin 7-engined specials built to the 750 formula. The company remained barely solvent by the sale of performance components to the 750 Motor Club fraternity for rallies and trials.

Chapman wasn't satisfied just keeping his head above water, however. He dreamed of a proper race car manufacturing business. The first logical step, saving the company both manpower and capital, would be to build a kit car which, with Lotus assistance, a customer could assemble himself. The customer would save money, too, since kit cars were exempt from the hefty British Purchase Tax. The concept was not new, but Chapman would develop the "do-it-yourself" car into an art form.

Lotus Needs A Winner

Chapman began, as is his practice to this day, by jotting down a set of general specifications for what would become known as the Lotus Mark 6. The car would be sold in components, including body, chassis, front and rear suspension, instruments, windscreen, radiator and gas tank. The car would basically be a sporting roadster suitable for competition in club racing. It should be equally at home on the road for touring or commuting, so lighting and weather protection would be supplied as well. Last, but not least, the kit had to be cheap. Chapman chose to eke out his profit from relative volume rather than single units. This first Lotus series production model also had to be a race winner—the future of his company depended upon its success.

Chapman decided on Ford (UK), rather than pre-war Austin (his earlier preference), as the source for engine, transmission and brakes. At the time, both new and secondhand parts were plentiful and inexpensive. To take advantage of volume production, normal manufacturing procedure would have been to make all the kits identical. Chapman, however, was always happy to oblige a customer by modifying a car—for the right price. Consequently, Lotus kit history is somewhat confused by factory-special or extra equipment that appeared on some cars but not on others.

Landmark Design

Colin Chapman was trained as a structural engineer, so his decision to abandon proprietary chassis and design one from scratch was almost to be expected. Most special builders relied on the traditional twin-tube chassis with a separate framework to support the body. Chapman incorporated all load-bearing structures and body attachments into a true multi-tube space frame.

Such a method wasn't entirely new—the Italian Cisitalias had space frames in the 40's and the Mercedes 300SL had one too—but the Lotus Mark 6 was a landmark in British car design. Fully stressed and triangulated, the space frame's resistance to both torsional and bending loads was excellent. And, the bare structure weighed a mere 55 pounds. The Mark 6 space frame design provided the basis for every subsequent Lotus racing car until the development of the Lotus 25 monocoque.

The Mark 6 chassis was constructed of both square and round section tube varying from 1 to 1⅛ inches in diameter, depending on the intended load. The body panels were alloy and the undertray and cockpit

Mark 6 multi-tubular space frame was a first in British car design, providing the basis for Lotus racing cars until the Lotus 25 monocoque. This is chassis #48 (built in 1954), owned by Oliver Clubine of Ontario, Canada, during restoration in 1975-76. Fully stressed and triangulated, the space frame is made from 1-to 1⅞-inch square and round sectioned tubing and weighs only 55 pounds. Wire wheels are not original equipment.

sides were riveted to the chassis tubes to contribute additional rigidity to the structure. The nature of a space frame dictates rather high body sides, and while a disadvantage in some cars because of the high door sills, the Six was so low that doors were unnecessary.

Construction of this advanced space frame was farmed out to the appropriately named Progress Chassis Company, a short distance from the Lotus works in Edmonton. Their fabrication methods were extremely resourceful. The welding jig was fashioned from an old iron bed frame, and chassis brackets were cut from any handy light gauge steel, including junkyard car bodies and surplus filing cabinets. If Chapman knew, he was determined enough not to care, and raced the car himself.

"Simple but functional" is the word for Mark 6 bodywork. "Egg crate" grille appeared later on Series 1 Seven. This is chassis no. 61, with the original Ford flathead engine, and is owned by Keith Spencer of South Wales, UK.

Simple But Functional

Chapman's specification for the Mark 6 included "simple but functional" bodywork. In terms of style, the best that can be said is that the shape looked like an evolution of the Lotus Mark 3. Aerodynamics were still another model away. To be fair, the Six did have a certain amount of flair, and the long hood line hinted at the car's purpose in life. For some reason, provision was made for spats to cover the rear wheels. The back end of the Six had compound curves and a finished look almost out of keeping with the rest of the body.

In back, the Six had compound curves and a finished look, as seen in this beautifully restored version owned by John and Jenny Chapman of Worcester, England (Chassis #44, 1954). *Photo: John Chapman*

4

Panel beaters Williams and Pritchard provided the alloy body panels. The kit included front cycle fenders, rear guards, nose cowl, bonnet top and sides, transmission tunnel, trunk lid—in fact, all the pieces needed to make the thing look like a proper automobile. There was space left behind the seats. A hinged trunk lid could be fitted for stowing luggage, or the well could simply be left open. Lotus Six sales brochures even suggested that a child "up to about 12 years old" could be seated there.

Suitability for the road was assured by the provision for a rigid or fold-flat Brookland's-style windscreen, wipers and folding soft-top. Headlights could be mounted on pedestals at the sides and back of the nose cowling, or inside the air intake. A bracket could be added to the rear bodywork to carry a spare wheel and tire. Not exactly sufficient to tour the Continent, but enough for a weekend run to Brighton.

The Chapmans' Austin A40-powered Six, soft top in place, looks ready for a fall run in the country. While not exactly aerodynamic, the long hood line hints at the car's affinity for the circuit.
Photo: John Chapman

Photographers To The Front

At the outset the Six was designed to use Ford suspension components, specifically the Prefect E93A series. Chapman had used a kind of swing axle on his Mark 3 and believed it a reasonable compromise in obtaining an effective, yet economical, independent front suspension. On the Mark 3 the system gave cornering power superior to the opposition and as long as the roll center was kept low, everything worked well.

For the Lotus Six, a Ford beam axle was transformed into a swing type by cutting it in half and bushing the inner ends. Ford parts were modified to produce radius arms and the whole assemblage was tied to outboard coil-over-shocks which figured prominently in the car's frontal appearance. Ford parts also supplied the steering column and box and all related rods and joints. In practice, the Mark 6 cornered very well, but the unusual geometry gave track-side photographers some really entertaining wheel angles to capture on film.

5

Colin Chapman cut Ford beam axle in half to create economical independent front suspension, first used on the Lotus Mark 3. The Mark 6 cornered well and provided good entertainment for track photographers. Outboard coil-over-shocks contribute to the car's singular appearance.

The driveshaft and rear axle were also Dagenham bits, with the axle located by a Panhard rod and the driveshaft shortened to suit the chassis length. Brakes were cable-operated drums of 10-inch diameter. They proved entirely capable of handling the car's light weight as long as the flathead Ford Prefect engine was used. Anything more powerful proved the rumor that Englishmen are more interested in going than stopping. On the race track the whole system worked nicely. The Mark 6 was basically an understeerer, but the car's all-up weight of under 1000 pounds was quick to respond to throttle (Chapman's car with twin SU's tested 0 to 60 in 12⅜ seconds), and oversteer could be induced at will.

Chapman Sets Limits

In 1953 special builders in England were notorious for their ingenuity in using a wide variety of power plants. However, Chapman elected to set realistic limits on engine capacities for the Mark 6. When the car was introduced, engine mounts were offered only for the Ford Prefect, Ford Consul and MG-TF motors. The first choices were obvious, while the MG engine at 1500 cc's was thought to be the upper limit in terms of power. Ford and MG provided a huge range of tuning services and accessories. It was rumored that a hot MG engine could pull the Six to 120 miles an hour! A wildly optimistic speedometer probably led to this tale, because aerodynamic limitations made anything over 100 mph unlikely. Nonetheless, as Lotus gained experience with the Six, Chapman agreed to offer mounts for larger engines as well.

By 1954 Chapman was offering the Mark 6 in two forms. The Basic kit, for "normal touring purposes," was set up for the Ford 8 (E93A) or 10 (100E) engine. Besides all bodywork and suspension, the car came with such amenities as Ford 16-inch wheels, speedometer, oil pressure gauge and ammeter. The Sports version, suitable for "mild forms of competition," was fitted with Lotus-modified, lightweight 15-inch rims,

Mark 6 amenities included tachometer for Sports version only.

tachometer and a variety of differential ratios. The engines were Ford 10, MG-TF, or the crème de la crème: a Coventry Climax overhead cam 1097 FWA (featherweight Series A). This new motor had been specially-ordered by a customer. The results, in terms of acceleration, were so sensational that Chapman offered it as the top of the line. In fact, the power and high rev potential were more suited to hill climb competition because of the aerodynamic limits to top speed.

The original cost of a Mark 6 is difficult to reconstruct because the customer purchased the car in pieces. Lotus supplied the chassis frame for 110 pounds sterling and the buyer took it from there. The set of alloy body panels (cowl, bonnet, fenders, trunk lid, etc.) cost £60 plus 15 for materials. Lotus would convert a set of front and rear axles for £20-plus. In 1953, *Autosport* told its readers that a fully-equipped Mark 6 with Ford 10 engine and all new materials could be had for about £425 (slightly over $1000).

Chris Smith drove his MG-engined Mark 6 for class honors in 1979 and 1980 historic racing in England.
Photo: Jim Evans

Six Takes The Track

The first race for the Mark 6 came on July 5, 1953, at the MG meeting at Silverstone. Second places were grabbed by the car's owner, Michael Allen, and by Colin Chapman. More important than placing, the car proved sound of design: there were no pre-grid dramas, nothing broke and nothing required changing. At the end of the first season, the first four Mark 6 racers had taken 47 awards in circuit racing, sprints and hill climbs, including 19 wins. The first Six to dominate club racing was Peter Gammon's, using an MG 1500-cc engine. In 1954 his record was 14 firsts, two seconds and one third from 17 starts.

Both Chapman and his number two, Mike Costin, raced the works demonstrator with good success. Their regular outings at race meetings served notice that this new Lotus Company was on to something good. The Mark 6 was not a world-beater, but a good, solid design that was competitive from the start. The Seven would follow in its footsteps before the 50's were out.

Restoring the Six

The Mark 6 remained in production for three years before making room for the Mark 8, the first streamlined Lotus automobile. When the last chassis was delivered in late 1955, around 100 had been built (the exact number is not known). Today the Lotus Six is a rare and sought-after model that deserves collecting and restoring. The continuing popularity of vintage and historic car racing in England and the up-surge of similar events in the U.S. have given a perfect outlet for the car's use. Although most engine and suspension components are obsolete, technical assistance can be obtained through the clubs and sources listed in Appendix 1.

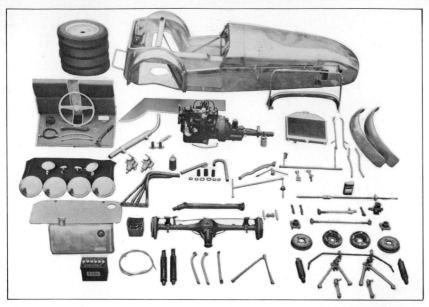

Colin Chapman elevated D-I-Y to an art form. *Photo: Spillman & Ramsay Ltd.*

Current owners report that the Six is a remarkably trouble-free motorcar. Problem areas are few. The Ford spindles and steering arms of the front suspension are prone to cracking at the base with long term use. At the rear, half-shaft or axle breakage is relatively common. Inspection of the keyway is vital because a failure here results in a wheel coming off.

The space frame is very strong and durable. Other than internal rusting or obvious damage from impact, the only frequent trouble spot is in the gearbox mount. Apparently the tubes that carry the mounting bracket are susceptible to cracking, so the fix entails removing them and welding new tubes in place with appropriate gusseting.

Gentlemen And Dirty-Nailed Racers

The Mark 6 established Lotus as a serious, if still specialized, motorcar company. Only insiders knew the operation was being run by part-time employees, including the chairman. Most of the work force was paid little or nothing at all. At the time, motorsport was run by and for a band of well-heeled gentlemen and dirty-fingernailed racers. Enthusiasm was enormous. Just to be considered part of the racing scene was the thing, no matter if there was any recognition or payment at all. They enjoyed their cars; they enjoyed speed and competition. It was FUN.

In the case of Lotus, the time and place attracted two men who would figure prominently in the future of Lotus cars. The first was Mike Costin, who was to manage Lotus affairs until his departure in 1961 to form Cosworth Engineering with Keith Duckworth. The other was Peter Kirwan-Taylor, who purchased a Mark 6 chassis and fitted a body of his own design. A lasting friendship with Chapman ensued. While never actually employed by Chapman, Kirwan-Taylor would lend a hand in the design of Lotus cars as well as unscrambling the company's financial dilemmas—roles he continues to this day. His most public contribution has been designing the body of the original Lotus Elite.

By the end of Mark 6 production, Chapman had guided Lotus into international sports car competition with some very sophisticated racing machinery. He didn't turn his back on the budget-minded enthusiast however. Even though Lotus mark numbers had climbed to 11, number 7 was reserved for the successor to the Six.

Chapman's instinctive sales genius, honed as he flogged used cars while in college, is evident in this very early (1953) brochure reproduced at right. Still makes you want to ring up the factory and place an order.

Can I . . ?

1.—Build a LOTUS in my lock-up garage ?
   Yes, even with normal hand tools and a bench ; no welding or machining facilities are required.

2.—Buy axles, engine and gearbox easily ?
   Yes, there are of course plenty of second-hand items available, but Ford and Austin main agents should be able to supply new components against special order as required.

3.—Fit a Riley 9 (or other engine) into a LOTUS chassis frame ?
   Yes, but you will need to make your own mountings—we can only fit brackets for the five " standard " engines. .

4.—Buy a LOTUS chassis with a door ?
   Either one or two doors can be supplied in any Mk. as required.

5.—Get some information about paying purchase tax ?
   Read the relevant articles in "Autocar" of 25.9.53 and "Autosport" of 2.10.53, which explain the position.

6.—Seat three abreast or have four seats in my chassis ?
   No, the frame design will allow only a small third seat—transversely in the back, suitable for a child up to about 12 years old.

7.—Visit the LOTUS Works—what is the best time ?
   Yes, anytime—please telephone first.

8.—Have a glass fibre body ?
   No, the present LOTUS frame is designed as a semi-monocoque unit which utilises stressed aluminium panels for part of its stiffness.

*The Motor
"... The preposterously fast Lotus!"*

WILLIAM R. CHUBBUCK
15 WASHBURN R.F.D.
Needham 92, Mass.

SHOWING ALL-WEATHER EQUIPMENT   OPEN TYPE REAR WINGS ARE OPTIONAL

LOTUS
Engineering
Co. Ltd.

7 TOTTENHAM LANE
HORNSEY LONDON N8

TELEPHONE : MOUNTVIEW 8353

★ Autosport, 2-10-53 ". . . I feel that the Lotus is the best attempt yet to provide the enthusiast with a competition car at a price he can afford to pay. In essentials, it is just as sound an engineering job as the most expensive sports car, and the economy is only brought about by the clever adaptation of mass-produced components.   J. V. Bolster.

FASTER THAN YOU THINK!

Technically . . . . Speaking

The **Lotus System** enables any enthusiast to build for himself a replica of a Lotus Sports Car, with the minimum of difficulty and expense. With this in mind all the separate elements are obtainable piece by piece and the actual assembly is a simple process needing little specialised knowledge or equipment.

The major unit is the chassis frame which is of semi-monocoque design and therefore extremely light and strong; it is supplied complete with all attachment points, including those for axles, suspension and steering components, engine and gear-box. The total weight of this structure is 63 lbs. The plan bracing of the frame comprises a sheet of high tensile light alloy rivetted to the underside which serves both as undertray and flooring. This has the advantage of giving a low centre of gravity with good ground clearance, effecting at the same time a great saving in weight.

Because of its integral construction the Mk. 6 body shape closely follows the lines of the chassis: so to assist the customer, and at the same time maintain the high standard of our

JOHN BOLSTER HOLDS BASIC CHASSIS FRAME   PHOTO AUTOSPORT

products, a set of light alloy body panels including cowl, bonnet top and sides, all wings and stays, propshaft tunnel, boot door, etc., can be fabricated to separate order for approximately £60, plus £15 for materials.

With regard to the major mechanical components, firstly the customer should obtain either new or secondhand a pair of Ford 8/10 post '39 Girling braked axle assemblies. From these it is necessary to supply us with certain components (see price list) for conversion to our specification. Secondly he should obtain an engine

and gear-box unit of a type for which standard engine mountings are provided (e.g., Ford 8, 10 or Consul and M.G., T.C. or T.D. Coventry Climax). If a different power unit is contemplated he must fit his own mountings. It will be seen from the price list that various other specialised components and optional equipment are available from our Hornsey works to enable the customer to carry construction through to completion easily and quickly. To sum up we can do no better than to quote The Autocar "... the Lotus is a very attractive proposition to those desirous of possessing a lively, small sports car at low cost but with the desirable attributes of good weather protection, simplicity, reliability and readily available spares from the world-wide Ford organisation."

Aerodynamic bodies of Lotus Mk. 8 and Mk. 9 can also be built to special order.

Most definitely recommended is our Mk. VI upholstery kit designed in conjunction with the frame for minimum weight and which, apart from the comfort, gives just that air of finish to complete the production car appearance.

Also on the price list are the Racing Components of which these items merit particular interest: (1) Lotus 15" Wheels which have three advantages: giving reduced unsprung weight, better gearing and allowing use to be made of the range of Dunlop racing tyres. (2) Special Close Ratio Gears for Ford 8/10 Gearboxes. (3) Special Crown Wheel and Pinion Sets of 4·7 (Ford 8/10) and 4·125 (1·5 Litre Engines) to fit Ford 8/10 back axles.

Competition Successes 1953 : First Production Year

In one season only, the first four Mk. VI cars to start racing gained **forty-seven** awards in competitive events—circuit racing, sprints and hill climbs—including 19 Firsts taken at the following well known tracks: Silverstone, Goodwood, Snetterton, Castle Coombe and Thruxton. Colin Chapman's car—chassis No. 9 fitted with a linered down (1099 c.c.) unblown Ford 10 side valve engine—has raced in many events at 11 meetings, took **twenty** awards and was never beaten in its class. Since then the cars have been even more successful, and in the hands of private owners more than 120 awards were won during 1954 by over 40 different drivers. It can be seen from this that success in competition is not confined to a few " works " cars and drivers, but is available to **all** LOTUS owners.

Main Dimensions of Mk. VI :
Weight with Ford 10 approximately 8·5 cwts.
Wheelbase 7' 3·5" Overall width 4' 3·5"
Track Front 4' 1·5" Overall length 10' 1"
Track Rear 3' 9" Scuttle height 2' 6·5"

PHOTO F. J. SMITH   LOTUS 1st, 2nd & 3rd AT SILVERSTONE

Performance Figures (approx.)

		STANDARD	MEDIUM	HIGH
Engine Ford 10	Degree of Tuning	(Normal Prefect)	(Limits of 1172 Formula)	(Special Cam, etc.)
	Maximum Speed	75 m.p.h.	88	94
	Petrol Consumption	45 m.p.g.	46	40
	Standing ½ mile	21 secs.	19	17.5
Engine Ford Consul	Degree of Tuning	(Normal Consul)	(Twin Carbs., etc.)	(Special Cam, etc.)
	Maximum Speed	99 m.p.h.	106	113 Plus
	Petrol Consumption	40 m.p.g.	42.5	38
	Standing ½ mile	18.8 secs.	17.4	16.5
Engine M.G.	Degree of Tuning	(Normal 1250)	(Max. of 1250)	(1500, Special Cam, etc.)
	Maximum Speed	104 m.p.h.	113	120
	Petrol Consumption	40 m.p.g.	42.5	38
	Standing ½ mile	17.8 secs.	16.5	15.8

2 Serie

Colin Chapman stands for publicity shot of Series 1 prototype. That's an Elite in the background. Both cars debuted at Earls Court Motor Show in October 1957.

: Birth Of A Legend

"The Seven was the car I dreamed about as a school boy. When I got the chance to build it, it was the most basic, lightest, high-performance little car we could come up with . . . A student's car, if you will—a four-wheeled motorbike."

Colin Chapman

By the time the Mark 6 ceased production in 1955 it looked as though Lotus would never return to producing a low cost, un-aerodynamic, dual purpose sports car. The Marks 8, 9 and 11 (the Mark 10 was simply a larger-engined Mark 8) had already been built and were extremely advanced, streamlined competition cars in all respects. Although similar in frame, the Eleven was as far removed from the Mark 6 in concept, design and purpose as a car could get. Nonetheless, word leaked out of the works at Hornsey that a development of the Six would be introduced in 1957. The new car would be called the Mark 7.

Many believed popular demand led Chapman to build an updated Mark 6. After all, a mark number had been set aside for such a car and there had been a steady flow of inquiries. The truth is, Chapman had planned a dramatic change for Lotus Engineering for 1957, and the Seven figured largely in his scheme. The year 1957 would mark the company's debut as a "respectable" automobile manufacturer. Chapman would build two cars to be used on the road. The flagship would be the new plastic-bodied Elite, and Chapman made sure the car would be the most technically advanced Grand Touring machine Britain had ever produced. But the Elite was expensive, and because of the car's radical technology, considerable development time would be needed before actual production could begin. The Lotus Seven would be used to fill in both production and price gaps. Based on an existing and proven design, the car could enter production immediately.

Contrary to some reports, Chapman intended from the beginning to build the Seven in far greater number than any Lotus to that time. As it turned out, both the Elite and the Seven were probably happiest on the race track, but the Seven would have the distinction of remaining in production longer than any Lotus car ever built. Ironic for an automobile Chapman designed in one week's time at home, and about which he today remarks: "I never had one for personal transportation and didn't have anything to do with the car after its production began other than to approve and test drive the newer versions. I really enjoyed the Seven in the early days . . . . I'm surprised it's still going."

Chapman Makes A Curious Acquisition

Chapman has stated that his initial concept for the Lotus Seven was closely tied to the Eleven Clubman: a basic car with independent front suspension and a solid rear axle. But while the car was still on the drawing board, a fellow drove into the Hornsey workshops to show off his Edward Lewis Lotus Special. Lewis had raced a Six and a Mark 9 with extraordinary success and decided to build a car for hill climbs and the odd club race. He'd salvaged a Mark 6 chassis; added a De Dion axle, Climax engine and a few other parts from the left-over bin. The car was bodied by Williams and Pritchard to Lewis's design and although it was "a bit of a cobble-up," it worked.

Surprisingly, Chapman offered Lewis the first Lotus Seven in exchange for this "cobble-up." Lewis agreed to a straight swap ("I knew that a car built as a special by Edward Lewis as a bunch wasn't going

12

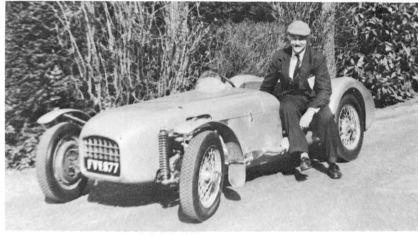

Two views of the Edward Lewis Lotus Special taken in April of 1957, with the proud owner seated on the car.
Photo: Edward Lewis Collection

to be worth as much at the end of the year as a car that Colin put on the road for me . . . "), but he used six works Elevens waiting for his Seven to be built. Thus was sparked a controversy that shadows the Lotus Seven to this day.

Many people have suggested that the Edward Lewis Special was in fact the prototype for the Lotus Seven. Chapman, however, has vigorously denied that the Lewis car influenced his design at all, and common sense would seem to bear him out. Colin Chapman was perfectly capable of designing his own car, without help from anybody. A more likely interpretation of events is that Chapman wanted the Lewis car off the street because he was afraid the cobble-up would make Lotus look bad.

Lotus Engineering Company was just stretching its wings in the mid-50's. While the Mark 6 had been favorably received and Marks 8, 9 and 10 were in competition, Lotus was still a back lot sort of operation. Chapman was uncommonly alert to any development that might adversely affect the company's fragile reputation. He likely thought that a sports car patched together from Lotus bits and pieces would harm the company more than it would help.

Lewis himself feels the only thing Chapman learned from the Edward Lewis Special was that the car had a ready market. "I think Colin Chapman . . . felt it would be better to get this oddball vehicle off the road and replaced by a purpose-built club car of a more thoroughbred nature," he says. "Colin at that stage was just beginning to get the bit between his teeth. He was going to be a manufacturer . . . He didn't want the Edward Lewis Lotus Special, which it was. He knew he had got to establish himself."

Edward Lewis eventually got his Seven, equipped with an FWA 1100-cc Climax engine and wire wheels. He entered numerous hill climbs and club races and was particularly successful on the hill at Prescott. Driving that Seven was "a unique experience" he remembers . . . "a cross between flying and super motorbiking."

The Edward Lewis Lotus Special, incidentally, was sold to an enthusiast in West Africa shortly after Chapman took possession.

Semi-Monocoque

The Lotus Seven chassis was a development of the Mark 6, but more closely resembled that of the streamlined Lotus Eleven. Various

Series 1 chassis closely resembled Lotus Eleven shown here, but Seven's space frame is of smaller diameter tubing (mostly 1-or ¾-inch) and there's less of it. *Photo: Adrien Schagen Collection*

economies had to be effected to meet the proposed low price range. Basically, there were fewer tubes in the Seven's space frame than either the Six or Eleven. The loss of triangulation was compensated for to some degree by riveting the undertray, transmission tunnel, rear body panel and body sides (flat panels that extended from the nose cowling to the rear fenders) to the frame. In effect, the Seven was a semi-monocoque.

Tubing was mostly 1- or ¾-inch round and square-sectioned 18-gauge steel, although some 1-inch strap and ⅝-inch square tube were also used. The square-sectioned tube was used in places where the chassis had to accept rivets or bolts, as in the radiator and front suspension bay. Lotus farmed out the chassis manufacture to Arch Motors. The firm held the contract through Series 3 production and even today produces chassis for the Caterham Seven.

One of the first Series 1 Sevens brought into the U.S. shows off its beautifully made alloy panels beaten out by Williams & Pritchard. While simple to assemble on the space frame, the panels were prone to loosen from vibration.
Photos: Ralph Poole

Keep It Simple

The Lotus Seven benefited and borrowed from the Mark Six. The Six wasn't so much styled as functionalized, and the Seven adopted an even simpler shape. The most obvious differences were the front and rear of the car. The Seven shared the squared air intake and egg crate grille, but the hood line had a gradual downward slope. The rear end lost the "sports car" curvature of the Six. In its place came separate fenders and a boxed section aft of the seats which allowed modest carrying space above the gas tank. The Series 1 tank, incidentally, was held in the chassis by bungee cords, making for simple assembly, easy removal for access, and spontaneous disassembly over bumpy roads!

The Seven followed its predecessor in that all body panels were formed in alloy by Williams and Pritchard. They were extremely simple in shape, compound curves appearing only in the nose cowling and rear fenders. The Series 1 didn't remain entirely alloy. Fiberglass fenders were introduced later for a special market.

The Mark 6 instrument cowl became a flat dashboard which also

Lotus Seven Testa Rossa

Peter Kirwan-Taylor enjoyed his association with the Seven and understood Chapman's concept completely. Still, he would have liked to add a little style to the automobile and perhaps tidy up the aerodynamics. The opportunity came when Chapman offered him a chassis to "play with." The result, as sketched by Peter Kirwan-Taylor, bares a startling resemblance to the pontoon-fendered Ferrari Testa Rossa. The forward fender has been dropped to nearly cover the front of the wheel, and extends back to join the rear wing. The headlights are molded in with long fairings. At the rear, Kirwan-Taylor provided curvaceous fender lines and a horizontal spare tire that doubled as a bumper!

Williams and Pritchard made the body out of alloy. While the car was admittedly more than your basic sports racer, Kirwan-Taylor's Seven certainly was pretty. The boss thought so too, but another stylish roadster was already on the drawing boards —the Elan. What Lotus didn't need was competition within the model line.

formed the Seven's scuttle. The radiator was well forward, which required the removal of the nose cowling to gain access to the header tank. Some Series 1 cars exhibit a circular hole above the radiator cap to enable topping up without the hassle of removing the front of the car.

Four over-center clips held the engine cover in place while the nose and dash panel were held by Dzus fasteners. The front cycle fenders were bolted to outriggers; the rear fenders directly to the bodywork. All components were designed with ease of assembly and maintenance in mind, but experience showed that whatever could vibrate loose inevitably did.

Follow The Elite

The front suspension was identical to the Lotus Elite double wishbone design, both having come from the Lotus Mark 12 Formula 2 car. Due to differences in track, however, only a few pieces such as the uprights, trunnions, and top suspension arms were interchangeable. The lower member was a wishbone of 1-inch diameter tube that located the coil-over-Armstrong shock absorber to the bottom of the upright. The upper wishbone was formed by the intersection of the top arm and anti-roll bar. The top arm attached to the upright by a ball joint. All pickups on the chassis and anti-roll bar were isolated by rubber bushings.

Following Mark 6 and Elite practice, Lotus placed the steering rack behind the wheel center line. The steering incorporated a negative Ackerman effect which meant that, in a curve, the outer wheel turned through a greater arc than the inner, giving easily-controlled understeer. At first the Seven used a Burman worm-and-nut steering gear. Shortly after production began, this was updated to the Elite rack-and-pinion, giving 2½ turns lock-to-lock. Front and rear brakes were cast iron drums of 8-inch diameter by 1¼-inch width. The front used twin leading shoes, but the rear was by conventional leading and trailing shoes to enable the use of a handbrake.

The Weak Link

The rear suspension was a live rear axle located by two trailing arms which picked up the chassis within the wheel well. A diagonal tube ran from the differential to the outer chassis to locate the axle laterally. All pickups were through rubber bushings for compliance and isolation of road noise and vibration.

Several proprietary axles could be used, including Ford, but most Sevens were fitted with Standard (Triumph) units designed for the Triumph Mayflower and Standard 10 passenger cars and station wagons. Production of the Mayflower ended in 1953 (four years before the Seven appeared) and the Standard 10 disappeared in 1959, but Standard must have made a bunch of axles, because Chapman used over 1500 of them until the change to the Ford Escort unit for the Series 3 in 1968. By then most of the spares were gone.

The Standard 10 rear axle was the early Seven's weakest link. Even with the smallest of engines, the car's cornering power was far superior to the lowly sedan from whence the axle came. That and the diagonal locating arm stressed the axle and differential case way beyond original

Double wishbone front suspension design came from the Mark 12 Formula car and is also used on the Elite. Circular hole atop nose cowl is for topping up radiator. License plate to the contrary, the Lotus Seven didn't arrive in Jay Chamberlain's U.S. showroom until 1958. *Photo: Ralph Poole*

Efficient front suspension was also inexpensive to manufacture. Sway bar forms forward member of upper wishbone, eliminating additional components and simplifying assembly. *Drawing: Paul Wasserboehr*

18

design limits, which resulted in anything from leakage at the differential seal to actual fractures in the ring and pinion banjo. (See Chapter 12 for suggested fix.) The rear axle proved to be one of the major drawbacks to racing any Seven.

The standard ratio was 4.8 to 1 but differentials could be supplied in an almost unbelievable array including 5.375, 5.125, 4.875, 4.55, 4.22, 3.89 and 3.73 to 1. Any customer who couldn't be satisfied with that selection probably didn't need one anyway. The rear suspension was sprung by coil-over-Armstrongs as at the front. Wheels were 15-inch diameter on 4-inch rims and were lightweight bolt-on. A spare was carried in a frame at the back of the body and secured by a leather strap.

The versatile Ford flathead was perfect for the kit car approach.

Engines For Everyone

Chapman remained true to Ford and specified their 100E, 1172-cc side valve (flathead) engine for the Series 1. With a modest horsepower rating (40 brake), the engine was ideal for the kit car concept. The 100E was readily available, inexpensive and most amenable to tuning.

The first Series 1 car, and several others to follow, differed markedly from Chapman's original concept. They were fitted with Coventry Climax FWA 1097-cc engines, De Dion rear axles and 4-wheel disc brakes, inboard at the rear. Although called prototypes at the time,

19

they were built for preferred customers. It is unlikely that much development data was gathered from these cars because the first was completed in late 1957 and Series 1 production was already in gear by January 1958.

These few Climax-engined Sevens made their mark, however, and other customers wanted the engines, too. Chapman was forced to abandon his allegiance to Ford and add the engine to his standard range. The disc brakes and De Dion axle were left off, though. Most Climax-powered Sevens had drum brakes and Standard 10 rear end.

SEVEN F

At the outset of Seven production there were three versions available. The Seven "F" used the Ford engine and Ford 3-speed gearbox. The "Basic" version had a 40-horse tune and gearbox ratios of 3.664 in first, 2.007 in second and 1 to 1 in third. The "Export" model used a tuned 100E utilizing twin SU's, 4-branch exhaust and a higher compression ratio. The 3-speed box was retained, but the ratios were changed to 2.34, 1.33 and 1 to 1. The standard differential was the 4.8. While optional on the Basic Seven F, a spare tire was standard on the Export version. Both models carried 4.50 × 15 tires front and rear. Wire wheels were optional.

Initially, the 1097-cc Coventry Climax was fitted only to Series 1 prototypes, but Chapman bowed to popular demand and added engine to line with introduction of Super Seven. *Photo: Sports Car and Lotus Owner*

SUPER SEVEN

The top of the line was the Seven "C" which used the Coventry Climax FWA engine (75 bhp). Also called the "Super Seven," the car had a BMC 4-speed gearbox with ratios of 4.08, 2.58, 1.66, and 1 to 1. The standard differential was the 4.5. Fifteen-inch wire wheels were standard (with spare), but the 4-inch rims carried 4.50 × 15 tires at the front and 5.00's at the rear.

The Super Seven came with a tachometer (optional on the other versions) and a 16-inch leather-covered, three-spoke, alloy steering wheel. The Seven F used an ugly 16-inch, two-spoke, white plastic affair supplied by Wilmot Breeden. It looked like it was taken from a Nash Metropolitan.

SEVEN A

In 1959 Chapman added another engine to the Seven line: the 948-cc

BMC four-cylinder overhead valve (37 bhp) as used in the Sprite, Morris Minor and Austin A35. This became the Seven "A" and used the same gearbox as the Super Seven C model. The standard differential in this car was the 4.2. The Seven A is not to be confused with the Seven America, which was a separate model added to the range just before the change to the Series 2 (see page 30).

The assortment of engines available for the Seven might appear confusing, but it made very good sense. The Mark 6 had started the tradition of using a range of engines to suit any pocketbook or purpose. The practice also enabled the owner to uprate his Seven as plans or finances allowed.

Bare Bones Indeed

The Series 1 sales brochures described the Seven as designed principally for milder forms of competition motoring—the ideal car for starting a racing career. Nonetheless, the car conformed very much to Chapman's original specification of a dual purpose automobile. A full-width windscreen was standard, but wipers were left to the customer's imagination. Headlights, fender-mounted side lamps, twin stop lights, rear license plate lighting, instrument lights and a horn were all fitted as well.

A fabric top and folding supports were optional as was a tonneau cover. The material was canvas or sailcloth. Sidescreens were never available for the Series 1 although resourceful owners came up with all manner of home-made alternatives. "Fabric doors" were added late in production to comply with the FIA sports car definitions. These were actually part of the tonneau that zippered—the center section could be removed, leaving the cockpit sides covered. They were probably most effective in preventing "7 elbow," an owner's affliction caused by constant exposure to the wind.

The final concession to touring was provision for fully-upholstered seats. The back rest was common to both driver and passenger and was not adjustable. The color, almost always red, matched the dash covering. That was about it. Bare bones indeed, but the enthusiasts didn't mind one little bit.

Time Filler

After the Seven debuted at the Earls Court Motor Show in London in October 1957, work began in earnest to develop the closest thing to a production line that Lotus had yet attempted. While the Elite gained applause and attention at Earls Court, there was indication that the car was going to be a hard sell. The average show goer didn't understand monocoque or half the other things the Elite was all about. Everyone, on the other hand, could understand the Seven. And the price, at £587 ($1643), they could understand best of all. A Morgan 4/4 cost $2195 that year; $2420 tuned up. An MGA could be had for $2750, a TR3 for $2665, an Austin-Healey 100/6 for $3195.

The works at Hornsey were bulging at the seams, even with Elite production taken down the road to Edmonton. The tiny shops were filled with the last of the Elevens and the Mark 12 single seater, and design work had begun on the Mark 15. Even so, every available hand was building the Seven kits and, every now and again, a finished and tested car.

Chapman wanted, and truly needed, a new, large, modern facility to begin his transition to specialty car builder. In October 1959, he got his wish. His friend Peter Kirwan-Taylor, the financial wizard, had arranged a million dollar loan. The facility was constructed in a new industrial park in Cheshunt some 14 miles north of London.

Line-up outside new Lotus works at Cheshunt (left to right): Elite, Series 1 Seven, Eleven, Mark 15 and Mark 16. *Photo: Homefotos*

Chapman took advantage of the move to reorganize his company. Under the banner of Lotus Cars, Ltd., he formed subsidiaries titled Lotus Components, Lotus Developments and Team Lotus. All staff were hired through a personnel office and the days of the part-time Tottenham volunteers were over.

The groups had different assignments, but all contributed personnel for the Seven line. Both Team Lotus and Lotus Components were involved in the racing program, the former campaigning works cars and the latter building customer "production" racers. As time progressed the Seven became a time filler for these groups, to be assembled during slack periods in their own programs. "Time filler" is misleading because demand for the Seven was sufficient to keep production going at a steady pace. Chassis lists show 242 Series 1's built from 1957 until the Series 2 was introduced in June 1960.

Kit Car Evolution

Chapman had learned much from the Mark 6 experiment and decided to take the kit a step further with the Mark 7. By that time several others had entered the "build-it-yourself" marketplace, but their products were basically what the Lotus Six had been—a bare chassis with a collection of body panels and suspension bits.

The Seven kit was much more. Everything that was necessary to put the car on the road was provided. The Lotus Seven was the first completely knocked down ("CKD") automobile. The body was delivered fully wired, plumbed and trimmed. Only the front cycle fenders needed to be bolted on. The engine and gearbox were supplied as a unit, leaving the suspension, driveline and cooling system to be assembled and installed. Even the nuts and bolts were packaged in canvas bags and marked as to what sub-assembly they were for. Lotus advertised that the average customer could assemble his kit in about 12 hours using common hand tools, and there was little reason to doubt it. There were problems, like the works forgetting one suspension side but packaging two sets for the other, or leaving a vital piece out entirely. Customers usually accepted the inconvenience with good humor. Such happenings were all just part of the fun.

Unusual sizes have always characterized Lotus sales literature. Seven brochure shown at right unfolds to 6 by 25 inches. It was published in 1958.

LOTUS SEVEN

LOTUS SEVEN SPECIFICATION

	Basic	Export	Super

LOTUS ENGINEERING CO LTD.

TOTTENHAM LANE, LONDON, N8

Telephone: MOUntview 1177 · Cables: LOTUSENG, London

Printed by A. G. Wood Ltd, Lancaster

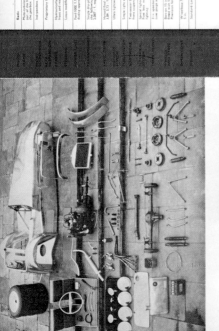

THE LOTUS SEVEN is the least expensive of the current range, but with a multi-tubular space-frame developed from the Le Mans winning Eleven, identical front suspension, the live rear axle mounted as in the Climax powered Eleven Club, the handling and roadholding are comparable with these incredible successful cars. The simple, practical body is reminiscent of the LOTUS Mk SIX but the mechanical specification is superior in every respect, particularly hydraulic brakes and rack and pinion steering. Many easily obtained proprietary components are used in the SEVEN and together with the straightforward design this makes it the ideal choice for the man who would like to build his own car.

SEVENS are available in three versions. The Basic, for the man who wants a complete car at a minimal price, the Export, also Ford powered, is mainly for customers overseas and has more extensive tuning plus many extras. Finally, the Super with an improved specification including an 1100 c.c. Climax engine, four speed gearbox, knock-on wire wheels, Rev counter and leather covered, light alloy steering wheel, etc.

ELIGIBLE for Ford Formula racing, the SEVEN provides an exhilarating introduction to circuit racing and can make an outstanding contribution for private owners during 1958 which provides promise of success in this particular championship.

Seven owners have also won hill climbs, sprints and speed events throughout the country. An ideal car for the starting one's racing career.

Photo: Charles Dunn

VERY well placed, the instruments are complete, simple forms of comfortable instrumentation, ideal for the much favoured straight-arm attitude. Adjustable pedals allow for individual requirements of leg length. The remote gear lever being of calculated length covers the boot which provides useful storage space for small luggage, tools, etc.

EVEN though principally intended for the fine weather conditions the weight of the Seven never the less can be fitted with a neat hood. The supports stick folds away flush with the scuttle top and the hood can be folded away inside.

NEAT and functional, the SEVEN is extremely simple and can make exhilarating motoring car. Economy is an important aspect and up to 45 m.p.g. can be achieved on the road.

The works could not assist in assembly or the Purchase Tax agreement would be void. There was no shop manual, but Lotus allowed several magazines to publish accounts of how the assembly was done. These were copied and made available to buyers. Lotus encouraged a free check-over at the factory to make sure everything was in order. Most customers took advantage of the service. The factory issued certificates of safety after the inspection so that an owner could get his "home built" insured.

With the improved kit came a solid identity for the Seven. A Six owner had to obtain such a wide variety of parts to complete the car that the final result could be startling, if not disastrous. The Seven came with everything, so every car looked the same. This is not to say that every car was identical, because special equipment or slightly altered specifications were always confusing the issue.

The kit concept also assured the continuation of a money-making automobile. Chapman reckoned that the works could gather together the parts for a kit in a third of the time needed to assemble a complete car. He saved money and so did the customer. During the reign of the Seven, Purchase Tax on normal road cars ranged from 25 to over 40 percent, but the CKD car was exempt.

To Market

Initially, the Lotus Seven was sold only factory direct. Most sales were kits, but a few left the works fully assembled and ready to go. Chapman realized this sales method was not the way to enter the real automobile marketplace, so he began to sign up a small dealer network. The English "Lotus Centres" handled both the Elite and the

Chapman began establishing "Lotus Centres" for sales in 1959, as noted on this brochure published at the time, which emphasizes ease of building kit. It was!

Seven and could sell the latter fully built or as a kit. Some were more enthusiastic than others, but one in particular—Caterham Car Sales in Caterham, Surrey—would figure mightily in the Seven history to come. The Seven F sold for £587 ($1644), the Seven A for £611 ($1711) and the Seven C for just over £700 ($1960) all in kit form. This Lotus was inexpensive by any standard.

In America, Jay Chamberlain had been appointed sole U.S. distributor for all Lotus cars. The first Sevens arrived in his North Hollywood showroom in 1958. Chapman wasn't quite sure how the car would do in the U.S. and he pinned his hopes on the Elite, which was thought to be more in line with the buying trend of the Stateside enthusiast. As it turned out, the Elite very nearly closed the doors on Lotus for good; and America got its very own Lotus Seven.

Exciting At Any Speed

The Series 1 weighed between 725 and 900 pounds, depending on engine and accessories. With a power plant ranging from 40 to 75 brake horsepower, the car could move like a bat. Quarter-mile times ranged from 20 seconds with the Ford engine to 16.4 with the Coventry Climax—not as fast as the 13.3-second 4-cylinder Ferrari Testa Rossa, which was the fastest sports-racer around at the time—but not too shabby. Later in production, a Downton-modified BMC-engined Seven trekked the quarter-mile in 16.8 seconds, 1.3 seconds faster than the twin-cam MGA in 1958.

The theoretical top speed of the Climax-engined Seven with a 4.2 rear end was 130 miles per hour, but, like the Mark 6, aerodynamics limited the top end. Most Series 1's ended up with 4.9 rear end which

Costin And The Townend Ring

Open air touring was what Seven motoring was all about, but wind buffeting was considerable at anything over 35 miles an hour. Frank Costin, the aerodynamicist responsible for the body shapes of the Marks 8 through 11, once borrowed the Earls Court car and was annoyed to find his hair blowing in his eyes while his necktie waved at his nose. He immediately set about limiting turbulence in the cockpit.

Fiddling with the windscreen rake gave some improvement, but the real solution lay in an aerodynamic aid. Costin designed a kind of sectional Townend Ring (the cowling around radial piston aircraft engines) which he attached to the sides and top of the windscreen. Once the air foils were adjusted, he could drive at any speed and his hair and tie would blow perfectly rearward. Chapman, evidently, believed if you drove a Seven you ought to look like you'd been driving one (either that or wear a cap and a tie clip). He discarded both the idea and the device.

Frank Costin today—still pursuing aerodynamic perfection. *Photo: Dennis Ortenburger*

25

held top speed to slightly better than 80 miles per hour. Of course, any speed was bound to be exciting in a car low enough to touch the ground with the palm of your hand. Getting there was the fun and lighting up the tires was easy in a stop light grand prix.

The other half of Seven motoring was going around corners and the car could do that as if on rails. Early road tests even suggested hill climbs and sprints as ideal competition outlets for the car. The Seven's ride was rough as a Morgan with bad shocks, but the low center of gravity and well-controlled suspension contributed to its tenacious cornering power. When Chapman discarded the Burman steering box for his own rack-and pinion, the steering lived up to the rest of the car's performance. Although Chapman intended world-wide sales there is no evidence that the Series 1 was ever built in left-hand drive. (A special version was produced for the U.S. market; see page 30 .)

Stopping was in keeping with going, even with the small drum brakes. Most testers criticized the hand brake, however, because of its awkward horizontal location above the left hand footwell.

Chapman designed the Seven's interior space with the height of the average Englishman (himself) in mind. As a result, if the customer was 5 feet 9 inches tall he would fit. If he wasn't, he wouldn't. Non-adjustable seats didn't help. The phenomenon was that if you wanted one badly enough you could somehow wear it.

Getting into the Seven was relatively easy if you were the passenger. The driver had to straddle the steering wheel and wriggle himself in. With the top up, entering a car that has no doors is remarkably akin to crawling through the windowspace. In the Seven, the experience was humiliating at best. *Sport Cars Illustrated* likened the sensation to "climbing into a frozen sleeping bag with a wooden leg." To avoid passer-by laughter, the accepted drill was to unsnap one corner of the top

Away from prying eyes, Don Pisor shows how to get into a Lotus Seven without unsnapping the top. *Photos: John Lamm*

Mike Addington rounds the hay bales in a
1959 Ford-powered Series 1 Seven.

and casually drop into place. Once snugged into the pilot seat, you could
reach around and button the top back up. The top, incidentally, had no
special sealing around the windscreen and was held in place by myriad
post and eye snaps.

In rainy weather a Seven driver had to dress for the occasion as the
water came in everywhere. The cycle fenders kept most of what was
being thrown by the front wheels in check, but a spattered right elbow
was a Seven owner's trademark.

On The Circuit

Power to weight is one of the primary considerations when selecting a
race car and the Lotus Seven provided the ideal combination. With the
Seven A capable of 0 to 60 in 12 seconds and the C rocketing there in
under 9, the car was a natural for competition. Predictably, the first
outings were hill climbs. In 1958 and 1959, Seven C's captured first
places no less than three times in the 1100-cc class at the Bugatti Owner's

Club meetings at Prescott. The Seven performed similarly at the BARC climbs at Brunton and Firle and the hills at Shelsley Walsh and Great Auclum. The Series 1 took to the circuits as well and class wins came at virtually all the English club circuits. By 1959 the Seven F dominated the 1172 Formula class while the C was acknowledged king of the sprints.

Keith Hamblin gets ready to attack Firle Hill Climb. Years later, this car would be modified and renamed the "Lotus 7½" (see Chapter 9). *Photo: Duncan Stewart Collection*

Wire-wheeled Series 1 on Easter Sunday at Goodwood, 1959. *Photo: London Art Tech*

1960 was the Lotus Seven high point in 1172 racing. The annual Chapman Trophy was awarded to Jeremy Cottrell for two wins at Oulton Park and one each at Snetterton and Silverstone; two seconds at Silverstone and one at Oulton; and thirds at Brands Hatch, Aintree, Snetterton and Silverstone.

Other finishers in the Chapman Trophy series that year were: M. F. Goodwin—4th, T. M. D. Dixon—9th, and Jon Derisley and J. J. Hall—tied for 11th.

C.M. Clairmonte pushes past Horace Gould in Cooper MG to finish second at Midlands Motor Club meet, June 1953. Following are two Lester MG's and Frazer Nash Le Mans Replica.
Photo: Tim Parker Collection

The Original Mark Seven

In early 1953, just as development was beginning on the Six, Chapman received an inquiry from two brothers by name of Clairmonte. Impressed with the trials and circuit racers built by Lotus Engineering Company, they wondered if Chapman could design a Formula 2 car for them. The proposal was for Lotus to design the body, chassis and suspension for which they would provide an ERA engine and suitable gearbox.

Chapman agreed because he figured the project might be a ticket into big time racing. If successful, there would obviously be a market for replicas. The Clairmontes didn't care what the car was named—all they wanted was a Colin Chapman design—but to suit Chapman's plan it had to be called a Lotus. Since the next model designation was Seven, the Hornsey drawing boards were coded *Lotus MK. 7 Formula II car.*

Apparently the project soured shortly after con-struction began on the prototype. Perhaps the Clairmontes didn't have sufficient financial backing or their organization was not up to standards. Or, maybe Chapman felt the car was too much too soon. What is known is that a rolling chassis was completed and delivered. When Chapman learned that the ERA engine had blown up before installation, he used the occasion to withdraw from the project and take his name and his mark number with him. The number "seven" was then set aside for the successor to the Six.

The Clairmontes completed the car but with a significant alteration to the chassis and a body of their own design. The "Clairmonte Special" was run as a sports car with a Lea Francis engine. With a Chapman space frame, double wishbone front suspension and a De Dion axle at the rear, the car would make for some interesting comparisons today. (Wonder if the Special still exists?)

Elongated fiberglass "clam shells" first appeared on Series 1 Seven America, so named because it was specifically configured to help capture more sales in the United States. At the time (late 1959) it offered the most performance per dollar in the U.S. *Photo: William Bradley*

The Seven America

In late 1959 Jay Chamberlain asked Chapman to do a special version of the Seven for the American market. Some resistance had been felt in the U.S. over the options list. Chamberlain thought that a tachometer, top, tonneau and even wire wheels were mandatory if the car was to sell. For the Seven to conform at all with domestic regulations there had to be sealed beam headlights, turn indicators and, yes, windshield wipers. There was something about those cycle fenders, too, in that Americans associated them with hot rods . . . and in the late 1950's hot rods and sports cars were thought to be worlds apart (driven by wild-eyed maniacs on the one hand, effete dilettantes on the other, depending upon one's point of view).

Chapman obliged, not wanting to hurt a potentially significant market and announced the Lotus Seven America. Contrary to much that has been written, this was still a Series 1 Seven. Chamberlain got his tach, top and tonneau. The Seven America also came with the FIA fabric doors (but still no sidescreens) and even had carpets and a spare tire. Wire wheels remained optional. A manually-actuated electric fan, which was being fitted with increasing regularity to English Sevens, was also standard. Theoretically, any of the three engines available in England could have been used, but most Americas were shipped to the U.S. with the BMC unit. The car's proper nomenclature thus became "Lotus Seven A America."

The most dramatic change was the front fenders. The distinctive cycle fenders grew into elongated fiberglass clam shells. The rear fender was slightly flattened as well, to hug the tire. John Frayling, the master clay modeler responsible for the full scale Elite mockup, designed and sculpted the shapes, and the molding was done at Cheshunt.

Turn indicators were perched MG-style (they were in fact MG in origin) on the tops of the front fenders—this Seven looked like a chopped and channeled MG-TC. Separate turn signals and stop lights were added to the backs of the rear fenders.

The Seven America could be acquired as a kit, but many were assembled by the dealers prior to sale. The dealers had good reason to import the cars as kits—the duty was less for car parts than for a whole automobile and the savings could be passed on to their own pocketbooks. Even so, with a sticker price of $2897, the Seven America offered the most performance per dollar available in the United States.

Edward Lewis in a Series 1 tackles the Shelsley Walsh hill climb in 1957. *Photo: J.H. Cuff*

30

3 Ser and C

This magnificently restored Super Seven
Cosworth 109E is the pride of
Bill Wade of New South Wales, Australia.
Photo: Owen Wuillemin

In October 1959, Chapman hosted the grand opening celebration for his new factory at Cheshunt. Over 200 guests traipsed through the spacious, modern facility north of London. All agreed Lotus finally had a plant befitting a winning race car operation.

The Series 1 Seven was selling well and performing marvelously on the track. But Chapman, being a good businessman, wanted to consolidate his position by making the car less expensive and easier to produce. Both would be facilitated by the move to Cheshunt. Chapman also wanted a subtle change in philosophy. The Mark 6 had been a competition car that could be driven on the street. The Series 1 Seven was a beginner's competition car. The next Seven would be a road car—at home on the track. Thus conceived, the Series 2 Seven was born in June of 1960.

Simplify, Simplify

The Series 2 was accompanied by much fanfare about a completely redesigned frame. What Lotus actually did was to conduct an exercise to see how many tubes could be removed before the chassis collapsed under its own weight. Just short of that point, the alloy side panels, undertray, transmission tunnel and rear body panel were riveted in place to restore rigidity. As in the Series 1, the chassis tubes were mostly 1- or ¾-inch round and square sectioned steel, with ⅜-, ½- and ⅝-inch used for suspension pickups and minor chassis members.

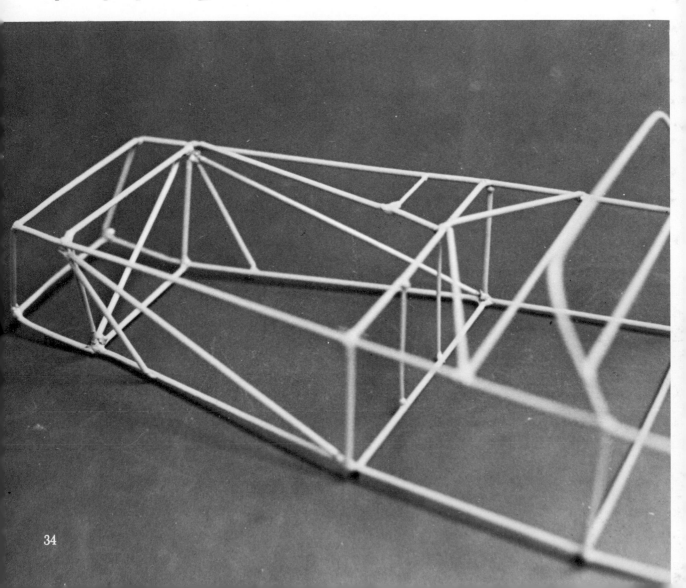

The Series 2 chassis economies made themselves known by routine failure, especially when larger, more powerful engines were fitted. The most common breakage occurred in the forward bay that picked up the suspension. There was no triangulation; simply an open rectangle of 1-inch square tubing. Brackets on the top section located the upper suspension components. The lower A-arm was bolted to a ½-inch tube welded into a hole in the chassis member. Braking and cornering loads caused the chassis rectangle to lozenge. Eventually, either the bracket or the intersect of the vertical and horizontal chassis tubes broke. In American racing, the failures were so common the SCCA encouraged drivers to add two diagonal and two horizontal tubes to the suspension bay. The four new tubes didn't stop the cracking, but they did enable a tow truck to remove a disabled Seven without damaging the front of the chassis.

A pair of Series 2 space frame models built by Jim Gallagher (see Chapter 11) illustrate Chapman's cost-cutting redesign of the Series 1 space frame. At left is a close-up of the original engine bay, and below is the strengthened version as done by Gallagher to prevent chassis flexing and subsequent breakage. *Photos: Dennis Ortenburger*

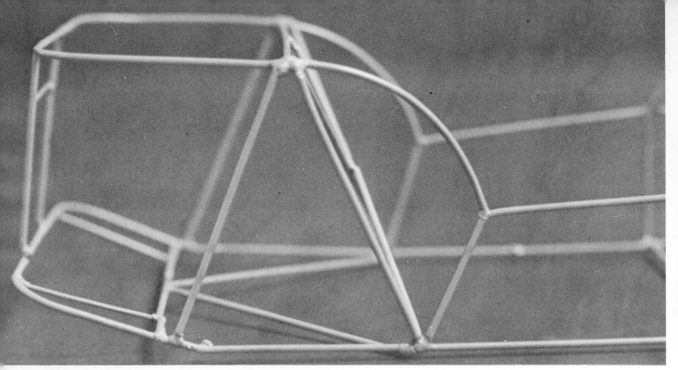

A rear view of the Gallagher model. The unsupported vertical tube at near right is a prime weak spot, as clearly shown in photo of one which has cracked and broken free.
Photo: Dennis Ortenburger

Another area that sooner or later gave way was the chassis location for the rear trailing arms. The forward end of the arm was bolted to a ⅜-inch (inner diameter) sleeve welded into a 1-inch vertical chassis tube. Because the pickup was in the middle of the unsupported tube, the resultant bending action caused the sleeve to oval. In extreme cases, the tube itself would break.

The transmission mount suffered as well from the increased torque loads of the more powerful Series 2 car. Steel sheet was angle-bent and welded to form a cradle mount that was riveted to the alloy tunnel. Although a rubber pad separated the mount from the gearbox, long-term load effects stretched the rivets, allowing the mount to move about and, eventually, crack the tunnel.

These weaknesses were bothersome, but not crippling. Enthusiastic Seven-owners have carefully worked out fixes for each. See Chapter 12 for details.

Compare "droop snoot" Series 1 with squared-off Series 2
of Frayling/Kirwan-Taylor design. Third in line is a Lotus Eleven.

Bonnets Take Flight

In shape, the Series 2 was simply an evolution of the Series 1, but the
differences were readily apparent. The alloy nose cowling lost its
downward slope to become a squared snout continuous with the hood
line. John Frayling designed the nose with Peter Kirwan-Taylor and
later shaped the fiberglass molds. The front egg crate that gave the
Series 1 a kind of gaping look was replaced by a barbecue grille of more
conventional design.

This original 1961 Seven America shows new barbecue grille and fiberglass
clam shells. Front license plate bracket was later standard for all models.
Series 1 radiator filler cap has disappeared. *Photo: Road & Track*

The clam shells were judged better looking than the cycle fenders and ultimately were fitted on all Sevens. Series 2 wheels were 13- instead of 15-inch, with wire wheels no longer an option.
Photo: Road & Track

Initially, alloy front cycle fenders were standard on all English Sevens while fiberglass "clam shells" graced the Seven America. The fiberglass numbers were definitely more effective in deflecting road debris. General opinion held they were better looking, in the bargain. Ultimately, popular demand led to their being fitted on all Sevens, whether for export or home market.

The engine cover, scuttle and rear panel were similar to Series 1 versions and were made of alloy. Over-center clips held the bonnet to the body sides. Unfortunately, the fasteners lost tension with time and use and spontaneous bonnet flights became a frequent topic of conversation among Seven drivers.

Scrub Negative Ackerman

The Series 2 front suspension was the twin of the Series 1's, with one significant difference: the steering rack was moved ahead of the wheel center line. This relocation signaled the end of the Seven's negative Ackerman effect and followed Chapman's thinking on the latest Lotus formula cars. The negative Ackerman had given superb high speed tracking, accompanied by a significant degree of scrub in low speed turns. The new position allowed the front wheels to toe out in cornering. The rack was changed to the Triumph Herald unit which gave 2¾ turns lock-to-lock.

Initially, drum brakes were specified at all four wheels: 8″ × 1¼″ fronts and 7″ × 1¼″ rears. In 1962, 9½-inch diameter Girling discs were

KAR 120C: The Most Famous Seven

The Lotus Seven Series 2 that wore the English registration number "KAR120C" may be the most famous Seven of all time. Not because it won the most races, or had any peculiar specification. It was in fact, quite an ordinary car. Except for one thing—millions of television viewers saw this Seven every week in the opening scenes of "The Prisoner."

Patrick McGoohan would come blasting toward spy headquarters through surrealistically empty London streets and then roar off to new adventures. Not since Emma Peel and her Lotus Elan quickened our pulse (for more than one reason) has television watching been as much fun.

Photo: ITC Entertainment

39

fitted at the front in the Super Seven range. The rear drums used special M.S. 3 linings. Wheels on all models were reduced from 15 to 13 inches in diameter, with 3½-inch Triumph rims. Later, tire developments allowed rim widths of 4½ to 5 inches. Wire wheels were dropped from the options list.

The rear suspension featured the Standard (Triumph) live axle, modified to lower the roll center. The diagonal tube that connected differential to outer chassis on the Series 1 was replaced with a wide-based A-bracket that picked up the lower chassis near the parallel locating arms. The point of the "A" attached to the bottom of the differential. All linkups were through rubber bushings.

Except for placement of steering rack, front suspension was twin of the Series 1's. Note Lucas driving lights on this original Series 2: pencil beam (right) and wide angle (left). Windshield wipers and manually-controlled electric radiator fan were standard on Series 2.
Photo: Adrien Schagen Collection

Rear suspension as used on Series 2 and 3 models. Chapman's efficiency is again evident in the simplicity of this design. Lower A-frame acts as both lower trailing arms and lateral locating device. Arrows show drawback to this system: a torque load path which highly stresses rear axle housing. Note large reinforcement plate to prevent axle breakage.
Drawing: Paul Wasserboehr

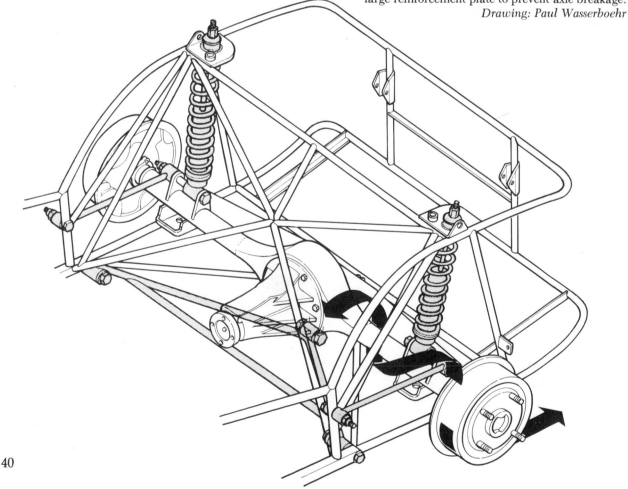

The effect of the modification was to make the Series 2 a better-handling, but weaker, Seven. The A-bracket did a good job of locating the axle, but contributed even more stress to the differential housing. As the car acquired more powerful engines and wider tires, the rear end was stressed way beyond the original design range. A new failure was added to the list: half-shaft breakage (see Chapter 12).

Dizzying Array of Engines

The Series 2 was characterized by a dizzying array of engine and gearbox combinations. Over the eight-year production span, Lotus managed to more than double the car's horsepower. Despite Chapman's initial intentions, the Seven was turning into little short of a wheel-standing dragster.

BMC (SEVEN "A" AND SEVEN AMERICA)

In the beginning were the 948-cc BMC series "A" engine (Sprite) and the 1172-cc Ford 100E Series "F". The Coventry Climax option was dropped—allegedly, because it was no longer suitable for the chassis. In fact, the motor was too expensive for the kit car concept. The Sprite was a good choice because the engine was almost unbreakable in stock form. The line of available tuning accessories read like a telephone directory. As the BMC increased in capacity from 948 to 1100-cc's, the updates were made available for the Seven A. On paper, there were subtle differences between home and export engines. The English BMC (948-cc) carried a 4-branch exhaust and a single SU for a horsepower rating of 37 brake. For export, twin SU's and increased compression raised the horsepower of the Seven America to 43 brake. In practice,

The virtually indestructable BMC engine with full Sprite options.
Photo: Pat Brollier

most home market customers opted for the faster motor. The gearbox was the standard Sprite 4-speed, but close ratio gear sets were available. Standard ratios were 3.63, 2.37, 1.41, and 1 to 1.

FORD 105E (BASIC SEVEN)

The Ford 100E side-valve (flathead) was specified on early Series 2 Sevens. The engine had peaked in 1959 in 1172-class English club racing, but Chapman wanted to maintain his ties with Ford. 1961 brought a free-revving delight: the compact, overhead-valve Ford 105E, as used in the new Anglia sedan. Like the side-valve, the 105E was a four-banger, but with a 997-cc capacity. This engine was available with twin SU's or a single Weber 40-DCOE side draft and developed about 50 horsepower with the 4-branch exhaust manifold. The 105E was treated to a wide range of tuning accessories.

The gearbox was the Anglia 4-speed; the first all-synchro box fitted to the Seven. Ratios were 4.118, 2.396, 1.412 and 1 to 1. The close ratio alternative gave 2.917, 1.696, 1.28 and 1 to 1. There was a problem, however, with the close ratio box. The gearsets were specially modified by machining away the first motion gears and welding on the close ratio set. The heat treatment was never quite right and the gears had a reputation for premature wear.

Lotus apparently had their fill inventorying differentials with the Series 1. The 4.55 was standard on both the Ford- and BMC-powered Series 2's, with only the 4.11 and the 4.875 listed as options.

The 105E became the basic Series 2 Seven, replacing the BMC-engined Seven A. At the same time, the "Seven America" designation was dropped because there were no longer significant differences between home and export models.

FORD 109E SUPER SEVEN

Chapman had given the Series 1 a Super Seven variant almost immediately, but the Series 2 had to wait until January 1961. The Series 2 Super Seven was the Cosworth-modified Ford 109E, as used in stock form in the Ford Classic sedan. The engine displaced 1340 cc's, and, with dual 40-DCOE Weber carburetors, 4-branch exhaust system and Cosworth head-work, put out 85 brake horsepower. The Cosworth alloy valve cover made the motor look good, too.

The engine modifications transformed the car into a real screamer with impressive torque output. The 109E in Cosworth tune developed 80 foot pounds at 4000 rpm which made this Seven the fastest-accelerating version yet (0 to 60 in 9.9 seconds). The Ford Classic gearbox spoiled things, though. Galling on the first- and second-gear sliding splines made quick shifting possible only if you could stand the noise. The specified differential was a longer-legged 4.11, but the optional 4.5 was the one to choose for maximum acceleration.

FORD 109E SUPER SEVEN SCCA

The Seven market in America was becoming increasingly important. The car had made quite a reputation in U.S. racing and Chapman gave the nod for a special version to compete in SCCA events, appropriately called the "SCCA Cosworth 109E."

The engine featured full race preparation with twin Webers on Cosworth manifolds, 4-branch exhaust and compression of 10.5 to 1 (compared with the "normal" Cosworth 109E at 9.0 to 1). The head, ported and polished, featured Cosworth springs and valve train. The combustion chambers were modified. The bottom end used Cosworth pistons with selected and balanced connecting rods. The crankshaft journals were line-bored with steel main bearing caps. A high output oil pump, larger sump and close tolerance balance job completed the specification. Unfortunately, the Cosworth SCCA 109E was short on reliability. U.S. racers jokingly called it the "20 minute engine," since it would run just about that long before destroying itself.

For better weight distribution, the Cosworth engines were positioned further forward in the chassis. With driver in place, the results were a near 50/50 balance front and rear. (The Seven A distribution was 48% front and 52% rear). The change also meant the nose cowl had to be removed to pull the dip stick.

FORD 116E SUPER SEVEN

In September 1962, the Super Seven was updated with the Ford 116E 1498-cc engine from the Cortina. The official title of the car became "Lotus Super Seven 1500." Alas, confusion reigned. Customers could order either a "standard" Super Seven 1500 or a "Cosworth" Super Seven 1500. Both versions boasted an immensely strong, 5-main-bearing crankshaft. This development ultimately led to the extremely successful twin-cam version later used in the Lotus 23 and Elan road car. Years later, the twin-cam Ford came full circle to be fitted to the Seven.

The compression on the standard 116E was 8.5 to 1 with 66 bhp. As in the 109E, torque was significant with 79 foot pounds at only 2300 rpm. This Seven could pull its own trailer to the races! The engine used a single Weber 40-DCOE on a special Lotus intake manifold with a box stock cast iron exhaust. The delightfully precise and robust Cortina gearbox went with the engine. Normal ratios were 3.54, 2.397, 1.412 and 1 to 1. There was some variation, however, as Ford changed their specification. The close ratio box came from the Cortina GT and gave 2.51, 1.697, 1.412 and 1 to 1. A 4.11 differential was standard, but the trusty old 4.5 was still available if you really wanted to destroy the chassis.

COSWORTH FORD 116E SUPER SEVEN

The Cosworth version of the Super Seven 1500 used a special head with 9.5 to 1 compression, port and polish, and a high lift cam shaft called the Cosworth A11 grind. Twin Webers on Cosworth manifolds and a 4-branch exhaust netted 95 bhp at 6000 rpm and 95 pounds of torque at 4500 rpm. Lotus advertised the car could do 0 to 60 in under six and one-half seconds. It probably was a good thing the standard differential was the 4.11.

With six more years of Series 2 production, the possibilities for other engines and variants could have been mind-boggling. Fortunately for the writer, the Ford 116E was the last change until the Series 3 Seven was announced in 1968.

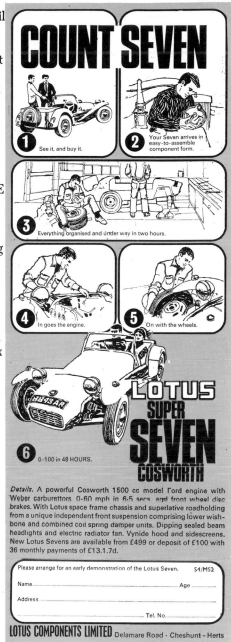

This ad appeared in motorsport magazines in 1962, touting ease of building a Seven.

Vroom! The Cosworth 116E used a special head, high lift cam shaft, twin Webers and 4-branch exhaust for 95 bhp.
Photo: Bernard Cahier

Lotus continued to add accessories to encourage street use. At right, frame for soft top is typically clever design: webbed straps fasten to top of windscreen to secure folding frame, then top simply snaps to body. *Photo: John Lamm.* Below, soft top is in place on original Series 2 with Dunlop racing tires. *Photo: Adrien Schagen.* Spare tire was standard equipment on the Series 2, shown at bottom on Bill Wade's restored Super Seven 109E. Top oval is taillight and turn indicator; circular stop light is beneath. Both are Lucas units. *Photo: Owen Wuillemin.*

One highly useful accessory marketed to help
domesticate the Lotus Seven.
Photo: John Lamm

The Joy of Touring

Even though the Series 2 was raced in ever greater numbers, Lotus
advertising continued to emphasize the joys of touring. Slowly but
surely, accessories were added to encourage street use. The folding top
and spare tire, optional on the Series 1, were basic equipment on the
Series 2. (*Road & Track* testers regarded the top as "a desperation
measure only.") Even more amazing, Chapman added windscreen
wipers to the kit—it must have rained once or twice in Cheshunt that
year. Tonneau and fabric doors remained optional except on Super
Seven models, which sported standard just-about-everything. When the
Super Seven 1500 came on line in 1962, rear quarter windows were
added to the top, which became vinyl instead of canvas. At about the
same time, hinged sidescreens became available for all models. Series 2
owners could order the Seven in either right- or left-hand drive. And,
the gas tank capacity climbed from five to seven and one-half gallons.

The Seven America was equipped with a front license plate bracket
(later standard for all models). For the first time, a heater was offered.
Lotus fitted a tachometer to all Super Sevens and Americas, but left the

Tony Caldersmith car-pooling again.
Photo Adrien Schagen

Caldersmith's Kidney Warmer

Tony Caldersmith, Cheshunt service manager,
car-pooled to the works in a friend's Lotus Seven.
During the winter of 1961 he developed that ail-
ment all Seven owners know too well: "frozen
kidney." With no further ado, Caldersmith set to
work designing proper sidescreens. The result was a
door *cum* side window that hooked to the windscreen. The design was simplicity itself. A pair of
inch-long sleeves were bracketed to the windscreen
frame. Corresponding rods on the sidescreen allowed for a quick slip fit as well as hinging. The
screens swung outward and upward to offer maximum entry room. Refined and color-trimmed, the
Caldersmith sidescreen became standard equipment on the 1500 Super Seven and optional on all
other Series 2 models.

45

gas gauge to the customer's imagination (usually anything that would serve as a dip stick). All Series 2 Sevens had rubber floor mats, but carpeting came with the Super series. Initially, the works supplied the old Melmac steering wheel, but a new Springall 3-spoke, 14-inch wood rim was optional. By the time the 105E was introduced in 1961, all Sevens had the new wheel. Even the manually-controlled electric fan became standard with the Series 2.

Springall 14-inch wood rim wheel was optional. So was the fuel gauge! *Photo: Owen Wuillemin*

Applying the term "standard equipment" to the Lotus Seven is a hazardous undertaking. Any customer could order additions or deletions to the basic kit according to his budget, needs or whims. Chapman was always delighted to oblige. Extra instruments, roll-over bars, limited slip differentials and special engine tuning accessories are only a sample of what sufficient money and patience could obtain.

Choice of body color is a case in point. The catalog listed sunburst yellow, tartan red, cirrus white, BRG and midnight blue as optional hues for nose cowl and fenders. The bonnet, body sides and rear body panel were bare (unpolished) alloy—unless otherwise ordered. Interior was red with white piping; top and sidescreens were black with red or white piping.

An annoying feature of all Series 2 Sevens was that the gas tank filler was located inside the luggage compartment. This meant the tonneau had to be unbuttoned to gain access and fuel could be splashed over the parcels or picnic lunch. Nevertheless, while hardly civilized, the Seven at least began to look a little more like a road car.

The Rocky Road

By the end of 1959, Lotus had begun to stumble down the rocky road to bankruptcy. It was the Elite's fault. The automobile was simply too ambitious for the fledgling Lotus operation. Production and marketing costs escalated until Chapman reported losing money on each Elite sold, despite the ever-increasing price.

In England, the Lotus Centre network was in trouble. In the U.S., the sole Lotus distributor couldn't move his cars. Word of the Elite's problems, real or imagined, had spread. That, coupled with the premium sales sticker, was turning buyers cold. The Lotus books showed a loss of $80,000 at the end of 1959, and the worst was still to come.

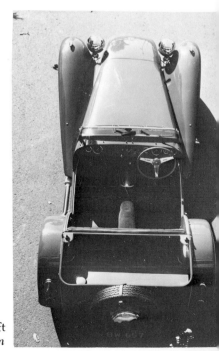

Bill Wade's restored Super Seven shows gas tank filler at left in luggage compartment. *Photo: Owen Wuillemin*

In late 1960, the American distributor, Jay Chamberlain, was ousted by his business partners. Lotus Cars of America went into receivership. All assets were frozen and cars were sold at wholesale to pay the creditors. Chapman had other worries, too. Bristol Aircraft called in the quarter-million-dollar note on the Elite body/chassis contract and Chapman didn't have the money to pay.

Now what??
Photo: London Art Tech

Kirwan-Taylor To The Rescue

A stroke of luck and Peter Kirwan-Taylor saved Lotus Cars from extinction. Kirwan-Taylor had been attending meetings between the Department of British Air Defense and the aircraft industry. The financial director of Bristol Aircraft, a car enthusiast and former head of the Bristol automobile division, recognized Kirwan-Taylor's name and invited him to discuss the Lotus situation over lunch. Skillful negotiation resulted in a plan of installment payments against the note. Peter Kirwan-Taylor had bought Lotus some time.

The pressure eased, Chapman did two things to boost sales: first he cut the price; then he went on the road. Viewers at the January 1961 BRSCC Racing Car Show were astonished to learn they could purchase the Seven kit, less engine and gearbox, for £399 (about $1100), factory-direct. A kit with the 105E engine and gearbox cost only £499. A real Lotus for $1400! Incredible! The home market came alive. Nine months later, Chapman announced the Elite in kit form as well, for a third less money than factory built.

Now satisfied with the situation in the U.K., Chapman took off for America to do something about the cars gathering salt on the Long Beach docks in California. His idea was to sell Lotus franchises to sports car dealers in major metropolitan areas. The appearance of some kind of dealer network might give a measure of confidence to prospective buyers outside the Los Angeles city limits. Chapman returned home with $850,000 worth of orders for Sevens, Elites and Formula Juniors. Lotus was in the black again.

Demand for the Series 2 was considerable, especially after the price reduction, and the Seven line was busy. Most of the work fell to Lotus Components, with Team Lotus lending the odd hand. By the time the 1500 was introduced in 1962, both groups had become so committed to other projects they could barely find time for the Sevens. "Immediate delivery" became a thing of the past.

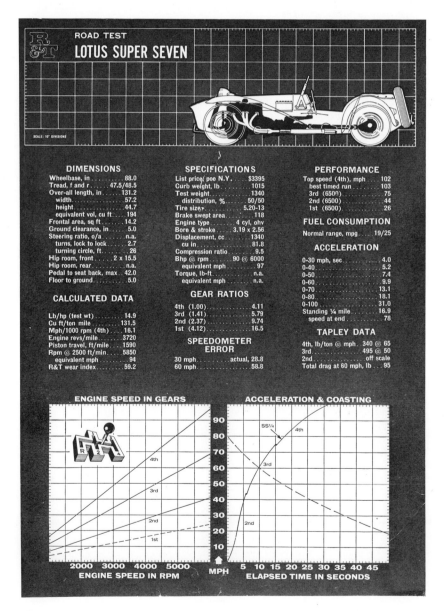

ROAD TEST
LOTUS SUPER SEVEN

SCALE: 10" DIVISIONS

DIMENSIONS

Wheelbase, in	88.0
Tread, f and r	47.5/48.5
Over-all length, in	131.2
width	57.2
height	44.7
equivalent vol, cu ft	194
Frontal area, sq ft	14.2
Ground clearance, in	5.0
Steering ratio, o/a	n.a.
turns, lock to lock	2.7
turning circle, ft	26
Hip room, front	2 x 15.5
Hip room, rear	n.a.
Pedal to seat back, max	42.0
Floor to ground	5.0

CALCULATED DATA

Lb/hp (test wt)	14.9
Cu ft/ton mile	131.5
Mph/1000 rpm (4th)	16.1
Engine revs/mile	3720
Piston travel, ft/mile	1590
Rpm @ 2500 ft/min	5850
equivalent mph	94
R&T wear index	59.2

SPECIFICATIONS

List price/ poe N.Y.	$3395
Curb weight, lb	1015
Test weight	1340
distribution, %	50/50
Tire size	5.20-13
Brake swept area	118
Engine type	4 cyl, ohv
Bore & stroke	3.19 x 2.56
Displacement, cc	1340
cu in	81.8
Compression ratio	9.5
Bhp @ rpm	90 @ 6000
equivalent mph	97
Torque, lb-ft	n.a.
equivalent mph	n.a.

GEAR RATIOS

4th (1.00)	4.11
3rd (1.41)	5.79
2nd (2.37)	9.74
1st (4.12)	16.5

SPEEDOMETER ERROR

30 mph	actual, 28.8
60 mph	58.8

PERFORMANCE

Top speed (4th), mph	102
best timed run	103
3rd (6500)	75
2nd (6500)	44
1st (6500)	26

FUEL CONSUMPTION

Normal range, mpg	19/25

ACCELERATION

0-30 mph, sec	4.0
0-40	5.2
0-50	7.4
0-60	9.9
0-70	13.1
0-80	18.1
0-100	31.0
Standing ¼ mile	16.9
speed at end	78

TAPLEY DATA

4th, lb/ton @ mph	340 @ 65
3rd	495 @ 50
2nd	off scale
Total drag at 60 mph, lb	95

ENGINE SPEED IN GEARS

4th
3rd
2nd
1st

2000 3000 4000 5000
ENGINE SPEED IN RPM

ACCELERATION & COASTING

90
80
70
60
50
40
30
20
10

SS¼ 4th
3rd
2nd

MPH

5 10 15 20 25 30 35 40 45
ELAPSED TIME IN SECONDS

Road & Track road-tested a Seven with Cosworth-tuned 109E in 1962. In 1961 test the editors found the Seven A with Sprite engine lacking in oomph. While this more powerful version lacked a first gear and seemed to be on fire at times (it was LHD so the exhaust pipe cooked driver rather than passenger), the testers pronounced it "one of the most inviting cars ever to fall into our collective hands." They were, however, mystified as to why the car was supplied with a heater.

48

The car could be purchased completely assembled or in component form. Lotus preferred the latter and most Sevens were sold as kits. Nonetheless, the shop men enjoyed assembling the occasional automobile because of the excuse to storm around the hills near Cheshunt. They fondly referred to their test circuit as "the mountain," and many a hair-raising tale originated there. Lotus advertising continued to quote assembly time as 12 hours and the reasonably skilled backyard mechanic could probably meet the challenge. With the Series 2, Lotus offered a six-month warranty on all parts. Of course, any claim arising from competition use was excluded in the fine print.

Anything But Greed

The factory did its best to keep Series 2 prices low. In England, the Super Seven 109E was available at £599 or about $1700. In America, though, the price tags bore no relationship to factory invoice-plus-shipping-plus preparation, or plus anything but greed. The Seven America (BMC engine) listed at $2925 and the Super Seven 109E at $3395—double the Cheshunt price. *Road & Track* called the 1962 Super Seven "shockingly expensive." Evidently, it was enough that the car was obtainable at all. As in England, the "four-wheeled motorbike" was gaining a surprisingly large following.

Inevitably, the cost of a Series 2 Seven rose in relation to changing specifications. The Super Seven 1500 (116E) that debuted in 1962 carried a price tag of £585 in component form or £868 ($2430) fully built. The Cosworth version listed at £645 in kit. As late as 1965, though, the basic Seven with 105E engine and gearbox was still available for £499 or $1400, the same price as in 1961. (The BMC version had been discontinued in 1962).

In 1963 the Lotus crew gave some thought to building an all-fiberglass Seven similar in concept to the Elan, but with a push-rod engine. Ron Hickman headed the project (code name "M9"). A study was made, a few basic sums calculated and styling sketches submitted. At length, Chapman decided the new Cortina project required their undivided attention and the all-glass Seven was shelved.

Enter Graham Nearn

By 1965, Lotus had outgrown the new works at Cheshunt. The industrial park had filled with small manufacturers and there was no room to expand. At the time, the British government was encouraging de-centralization of industry to develop outlying regions. Chapman took their advice and sought space in counties with no industry; hence, no union organization. He was well aware of the crippling effect of work stoppage and he wanted nothing to do with unions. A site was located at Hethel, near Norwich, in Norfolk. During World War II, the Hethel airstrip had been used by the U.S. 8th Air Force B-24 bomber wings. The surrounding area was completely agricultural. Chapman envisioned a sprawling factory, ready-made test tracks and room to grow. The move was accomplished at the end of 1966.

Compared with the Hornsey stables, the Cheshunt factory had been a model of industrial efficiency. The Hethel works gave Lotus yet another image. The plant was comfortable, air conditioned and spacious. The grounds were as well groomed as a championship golf course. Lotus was becoming a different kind of company. Later they would sell a different kind of sports car, too.

In the meantime, there was this cult that kept demanding more Sevens. Apparently, the car added up to more than the sum of its parts. Owners could not discuss the Seven without becoming emotional. Chapman was flattered by the movement to keep his toy alive, but annoyed at the production problems the Seven represented. Enter Graham Nearn of Caterham Car Sales, Surrey. Nearn had operated one of the original Lotus Centres set up to distribute the Series 1 Seven. Now, he offered to take over complete distribution of the automobile to separate the Seven from Lotus's upmarket GT products. In 1967, a relieved Chapman announced that Caterham Cars would be the sole Lotus Seven distributor outside the factory.

The Series 2 came to a halt in mid-1968 with approximately 1350 cars built. The eight-year effort created the most persistent following of any Lotus car, ever.

Going Like Blazes

The Series 2 Seven A and Seven A America with BMC engines were built until 1962 when the Ford 105E became the basic Seven. The Seven A weighed 960 pounds at the curb. While not yet scintilating, the car's performance belied 948-cc's. Zero to 60 times varied with the driver, but most scored in the 13- to 14-second range. Top speed was about 85 miles per hour. Gas consumption was very easy to live with at 30 to 35 mpg—not that Seven owners cared much about that.

Most testers said the Series 2 Seven A was stiffly sprung, but had excellent adhesion. The car was basically an under-steerer, but tire pressures could usually put the balance nearer neutral. Only on rough or wet surfaces was there any drama and then only if there was anything to crash into. *Sports Car Graphic* reported that on rough surface corners it was necessary to let the car drive itself. "It'll jump around and make a fuss, even hop over and change its line by three or four feet. If left alone, however, it'll wind up headed in the right direction and still going like blazes . . . " The unanimous conclusion was that the Seven was a tongue-in-cheek road car that really belonged on a race track. The 105E proved similar to the BMC in all respects. For many enthusiasts, they provided the best balance of engine and chassis of all the Sevens to date.

The 109E Cosworth, first Series 2 Super Seven, was a different matter entirely. The 85-horse engine (200 bhp/ton) pulled this car from 0 to 60 in just over nine seconds. The Super Seven could do the quarter mile in 15 plus a fraction, which put the Series 2 in respected company, indeed. Top speed was around 103 miles per hour. Most road testers didn't beat around the bush with the Super Seven. They said it was a race car, pure and simple. A lumpy idle, tremendous induction roar and fierce acceleration added up to the most fun anyone could possibly have in a car that was street legal.

The last engine fitted to the Series 2 was the 116E. The second Super Seven had all the power of the first, plus a smooth delivery. Top speed was the same. Acceleration, however, was in the 8-second bracket for 0 to 60. (Before you rush out to your car to prove or disprove these figures, please bear in mind that the numbers come from road tests of the period. They are offered strictly for historical interest.) If a Seven could ever be called "refined," the 116E was the one. Torque was low on the rev scale, while the car reached maximum horsepower at 6000 rpm. With the Cortina GT gearbox, the 116E was easy to drive quickly and one of the most satisfying Sevens on the road.

Now, if only something could be done about the side exhaust that singed every passenger on exit . . .

Raising The Dead

Since most Series 2 Sevens were raced at one time or another, the prospect of restoration is often dampened by a confusion of modifications. Faced with the utter simplicity of the factory item, some Seven owners let their imaginations run wild. (See Chapter 9 for some of the more interesting designs.) The original article, properly restored, is still impressive. For those who are wont to try, the clubs and other sources listed in Appendix 1 can help the most moribund of specimens.

Lotus wares on display at 1964 Geneva show, including complete Elan, backbone chassis and Jim Clark photo. *Photo: Wörner*

The Seven Days Were Numbered

During the years of Series 2 production, Lotus made giant strides in their Grand Touring cars and racing program. In 1960 Lotus scored their first Formula 1 victory (at Monaco), and in 1961 design work began on the Lotus 26 and the Elan. The Mark 19 sports racer was scoring international wins over machinery with engines two and three times as large.

In October 1962, the Elan was announced at £1095 ($3065) in kit form. The Lotus 23 debuted at Nürburgring with Jim Clark at the controls. And the first Lotus monocoque Formula 1, the Mark 25, won three GP's. The first World Championship to both driver (Jim Clark) and manufacturer came in 1963, with a record seven GP wins. On top of this victory came second and seventh places at the Indy 500. The Lotus Cortina was introduced. A "big banger" sports racing car was on the boards.

1964 was a lean year, relatively speaking, with only three Grand Prix wins. Clark lost the championship on the last lap of the last race. The Lotus 30, Ford V8-powered, proved to be a mistake. Only the announcement of the Series 2 Elan sparked Lotus fortunes.

The second World Championship title and win at Indianapolis came in 1965. Both the Elan Coupe (Mark 36) and competition Elan (26R) were announced that year. Another low followed in 1966 (only one GP win), but the Europa (Mark 46), Elan Special Equipment and Elan Drophead Coupe tickled the car-buying enthusiast.

1967 brought four GP wins, and no championship. But a new flagship was unveiled: the Elan Plus Two (Mark 50). Lotus was heading in new directions, both on the road and on the racing circuit. Refinement and luxury were displacing exhilaration. The days of the Lotus Seven had to be numbered.

4

Bill March at speed
in Australia in the mid-sixties.

Seven Goes Racing

Dwarfed by pursuing Corvette, John Morton shows the way at Dodger Stadium (Los Angeles), December 1963. Moved to B-Production by the SCCA that year, Seven was uncompetitive. Converting parking lots into race courses was a brief West Coast fad.
Photo: Dave Friedman

Colin Chapman may have created the Series 2 for sport motoring, but the owners knew better. They wedged themselves behind their wheels and headed for the track. The Series 2 was raced worldwide and was marvelously successful. The Seven ran as a production car in the United States and in various classes in Great Britain. But in Australia, the car created a new kind of race altogether.

England: Sprints, Hill Climbs And Road Racing

British enthusiasts took to the Series 2 in a big way and entered their cars in every possible form of competition. In the 1960's most class structures were based on FIA rules which grouped cars by engine capacity. There were exceptions, however. When enough Sevens registered, they were given their own race.

As amateur racing evolved in the 50's, there had been frequent reference to "Clubman" cars. The idea was a relatively inexpensive, yet reasonably sophisticated and competitive club racer. Clubman cars were required to maintain a dual purpose. They had to be suitable for street use as well as racing. All of Chapman's early cars were built to this formula, but the Seven was pure-blooded Clubman.

In England, many organizers offered amateurs starting money to help defray expenses. A driver could collect 25 to 100 dollars just to roll his car onto the grid. The amateur-Clubman concept worked well until the late 1960's when technology and outside sponsorship began to exert their influence. The name was the same, but the cars began to take advantage of the latest formula and all-out-racing car designs. The drivers were a different breed as well: no longer part-time club racers, but full-time professionals in search of contracts. The Seven will be remembered for ruling the Clubman class when there really was such a thing.

The Series 2 was a beginner's competition car. While some drivers made the grade to the big time, most simply raced the Seven for fun. The Series 2 was raced box stock or loaded with all available engine modifications. In the beginning, safety equipment was a crash hat and sometimes a seat belt. Roll over bars were years away. Some numbers and a Brooklands screen to replace the windshield were all that was really necessary. The Seven was your basic race car.

Only sprints, hill climbs and road racing will be addressed here. There were other forms of competition and the Seven was there, too. The car was entered in English mud sport (trials), auto tests and autocross, equivalent to American slaloming but on dirt or grass tracks. Through it all, the Seven was driven to the event, raced, and driven home again.

Sprinting At Brighton

The English sprint race of the 60's shared some aspects of American drag racing. Timing was measured by electric clocks to the hundredth or thousandth of a second. The cars were staged singly, in pairs or in groups to half a dozen. Courses could be a mile long and arrow-straight or three laps around Brands Hatch. Unlike drag racing, the lowest elapsed time won the race, regardless of how the winner might place in a pairing or group. Sprints were popular, low-key club events. Facilities were easy to arrange. If the local circuit was in use, any airfield or public road—even the beach front drive at Brighton—could be used.

In the early 1960's, the 1000-cc sports car class was dominated by the Seven A's with BMC engines or 7 F's with the Ford flatheads. A few competitors began to show consistent excellence, among them Jon Derisley, Roy Millbank, Harry Epps and R. Bell.

The Seven was a natural for hill climbs, too. Even the road testers said so. Power-to-weight, handling and balance were the essentials. While the event favored cars with large horsepower ratings, the Sevens were almost unbeatable in class.

The Seven took to hill climbs like a duck to water. Here, for example is Mike Addington in the wet at Westbrook Hay Hillclimb in 1961. *Photo: Craftsmen Ltd.*

The English were equally resourceful in finding hills to climb. Just about any grade that would keep a shilling on the roll would do. Timing was electronic and the cars were fitted with a vertical bar in front of the nose to trip the lights. In the early days, the Series 2 was triumphant at Olivers Mount, Catterick, Prescott, Ragley Park, Craigantlet, Castle Farm and more. Both sprint and circuit racers usually did well in hill climbs.

Jon Derisley: In The Driver's Seat

The British have a saying: "If there isn't a race, it can't be Sunday!" The words pretty much sum up their attitude toward motorsport. Nothing quite matches the excitement of direct competition in wheel to wheel racing. In the early 60's, Sevens appeared on club circuits by the dozens. Just about every successful driver cut his teeth on club racing. The club circuit was a stepping stone for some; an end unto itself for others. Two drivers typified the energy and enthusiasm of 1960's Seven racers in England. Jon Derisley and Mike Addington spent some of their best seasons driving Sevens in all types of competition.

Jon Derisley began saving his money for a sports car when he was nine years old. In August 1955, when he'd reached his late teens, he spent the stash on a secondhand Lotus Mark 6. The car was his only transportation, but he managed to enter one hill climb and six sprints

56

during the first year. Derisley frequented the 750 Motor Club meetings at the Abbey Pub and, inevitably, he ran into Colin Chapman.

Derisley was racing in the 1172 class and he asked Chapman for his advice on demon tweeks. The rules left few, if any, loopholes. Not surprisingly, Chapman had found a way. He told Derisley to arm himself with a micrometer and visit as many Ford dealers as he could to locate oversize camshafts! Apparently a few thousandths extra lift made all the difference, but Chapman suggested changing the cam after every race. Two seasons with the Mark 6 taught Derisley racing economics, perseverance and skill. Now for a faster car.

In 1957, Derisley acquired a Series 1 kit. In this car he began to make his name in club events. There were the usual surprises on taking delivery: missing bushings, top front suspension arms, seats and the like. On one return to the works for a needed bracket, the storeman excused himself and disappeared into the shop. He reappeared moments later, proffering the part with a pair of pliers. The metal still glowed red from the welding!

Derisley made only two modifications to the car. Each had a significant effect on handling. One was lowering the car at the rear by dropping the shock absorber mount, which made for more stable cornering. The second change was fitting a Lotus Formula Junior seat. Derisley claimed a second-a-lap difference at Goodwood resulted from the seat alone. With the stock set up he was continually afraid of being tossed out of the car.

Derisley campaigned the Series 1, and used it as a road car, for two more years. Chapman took notice of Derisley's fast and consistent drives and offered him a works Series 2 Seven in 1961.

This Series 2 was something special: a factory-built lightweight with smaller diameter tubes in the space frame. The powerplant was the Cosworth Ford 105E engine. Chapman told Derisley that he wanted a Seven to win the Brooklands Memorial Trophy. What he didn't tell him was that two lightweights had been built—the second car had gone to Mike Addington for the same purpose.

At Silverstone Clubman Championship, July 1961, Addington's Seven keeps just ahead of ex-works Aston Martin DBR1–250 driven by Baillee. *Photo: Harold Barker*

Mike Addington, in Series 2 with Ford 105E Cosworth engine (95 bhp), chases Keith Greene in Gilby Climax at Silverstone Grand Prix, 1962. *Photo: Harold Barker*

The first thing Derisley did was lower the rear end as he had the Series 1. The second thing he did was break a chassis tube (not the welds, but the tube itself) in towing. From there, the record speaks for itself: ten firsts, two seconds, two thirds, one fourth, one sixth. He captured five lap records with the car and was invited to join the British Racing Drivers Club (BRDC). A driver didn't get into the BRDC with a Lotus Seven no matter how many times he won, but Derisley was that good. He was beating the likes of Peter Deal, Piers Courage, Peter Gethin and Pete Lovely—all in Lotus Sevens. In the race for the Brooklands Trophy, Derisley ended up in a dead heat for first place with three other drivers.

At the close of the season, Derisley returned the Series 2 lightweight to the factory. Chapman promised him a works Lotus 23, but when the car arrived with a £2500 price tag, Derisley declined the ride. Instead, he bought Peter Lumsden's Elite, WUU2—but that's another story.

Mike Addington: Showing Some Verve

Mike Addington bought his first Seven in 1959 and managed numerous thirds and fourths in 1172-class racing. Addington's driving showed more

Mike Addington leans into corner racing at Mallory Park, 1961. *Photo: A. F. Fulwood*

verve than his initial placings would indicate. Chapman wanted him to have the second works lightweight car, but as an outright purchase. Like Derisley's, the Series 2 Seven fitted with a Cosworth 105E and Sprite close ratio gearbox. The first season saw lap records (in class) at every club circuit except Brands Hatch and Snetterton.

Just before the Brooklands Memorial, Addington crashed in a big way and the chassis was rushed to Hornsey for repairs. When Addington called several weeks later, he discovered they'd fixed someone else's instead. The lightweight was still in shambles. Mike Costin stepped in to save the day. Besides rushing the repair job, he made a set of wide wheels, converted the front suspension to dual A-arm wishbones and moved the engine further back in the chassis. Cosworth rebuilt the engine to the tune of 88 brake, which was something for a 1-liter motor.

Addington missed the 1961 Brooklands trophy, but ended the season with 26 wins. His biggest thrill came at Goodwood. He was the first 1000-cc sports car driver to lap over 90 miles per hour.

America: The SCCA

When the Series 2 was introduced to the United States, the SCCA was perplexed. The few Series 1 Sevens that made an appearance had been allowed to race as modifieds. In those days, the modified class in-

Lotus Seven shoots out of left field in front of Lotus Elite at Pomona CSCC, April 1962. *Photo: Dave Friedman*

cluded everything from true sports racing cars to altered production cars. The classification was pretty casual. No one insisted the Series 1 was a real car.

But the new Lotus Seven had factory documents that proved the car was series-produced. "Right," said the SCCA, "a production car." Ah, but what class? Of the several Series 2 engines, only one came from an existing sports car. By 1961, neither the SCCA nor the renegade California Sports Car Club (Cal Club) had decided where to place the misfit. The Series 2 ran in F-modified and occasionally (with fenders removed) in Formula Junior.

Finally, race officials bit the bullet. They put the Super Seven 109E in D Production and the Seven A America in G Production. This meant the Super Seven raced against Austin Healey 3000's, Alfa 1600's, Porsche 1500's and 1600's, Siata 208's, Turner Climaxes, Jensens, AC Aces and the like. The Seven America's competition was the Porsche 1300, Alfa 1300, Sprite (with full options), MG-TF, Fiat Abarth 750 and 850, Berkeley, Morgan 4-4 (105E) and Fairthorpe. Both Sevens beat everything in sight. Very embarrassing.

For 1963, the SCCA bumped the Super Seven two classes into B Production. The America was upped into F. Now the Super Seven raced against Aston Martin DB 2's and DB 4's, Corvettes, Ferrari 250 GT's, Lotus Elans, Elites, Mercedes 300 SL's, Osca 1600 GT's, Porsche Carreras and Simca Abarth 1300's. What happened? The car got beat by everything in sight. The Seven America won a few and lost a few, so F Production it was. Competition came from MGA's, Volvo 1800's, Mercedes 190 SL's, Renault Alpines, Alfa 1300's, Berkeleys and Turners.

The Super Seven was the problem. Hmm . . . let's see, too fast for D; too slow for B . . . It took awhile, but the SCCA figured out that Class C should be just about right. In 1964 the car raced in C Production against Elva Couriers, Alfas, Lotus Elans (several cars had been reclassified) Morgan + 4's, Porsche Carreras, Simca Abarth 1300's, Sebring Sprites and TVR's. The SCCA National Championships were run at Riverside that year. To participate, a car had to be a division champion or runnerup. On the grid were 11 Super Sevens, two Elans, one Morgan Super Sport and one TVR. The Morgan won and an Elan took second. Then came Sevens as far as the eye could see. The West Coast results for 1964 gave second overall to Joe Ward in a Super Seven; ditto Joe Demele in the Seven America. Classification for both cars remained the same through Series 2 production.

Too Fast To Race

All this classification and reclassification had not gone unnoticed by Colin Chapman. He wanted the Seven in production racing in the States; even gave the American racer a special SCCA 109E engine. The stakes were high. If the American racing scene soured on his cars, there went the sales curve. The SCCA didn't like the special engine because . . . well, *because*. The Seven had been a real headache. Many in the Club heirarchy considered the car a hazard because of its size. The blow-up came in April 1963, when the SCCA refused to accept the new Super Seven 1500 (116E) in either standard or Cosworth specification. "Didn't submit the necessary forms in time," they said.

Chapman was outraged. The paperwork on the 1500 had been sent in November 1962, along with specifications for the new 109E engine and the Lotus Elan. The Club listed the Elan and the 109E modifications for 1963. The Seven 1500, Chapman said, they simply ignored.

The SCCA responded in kind. The 1500 Super Seven did not comply with "the spirit of club racing." The 1500 Super Seven did not comply with FIA "bodywork" regulations. The fur started to fly. A flurry of official Lotus statements emanated from Cheshunt. The Seven had been in production six years. The Seven had been designed as an inexpensive racing vehicle. The Seven had given a number of prominent British drivers their start on English club circuits. If that didn't satisfy the "spirit of club racing," perhaps the SCCA would care to discuss the Ferrari 250 GT, the Cobra and the limited production Simca Abarth. As for the FIA regulations, Chapman noted that the SCCA had never paid them any mind before. The FIA classification was based on engine capacity. The SCCA grouped cars by performance, regardless of engine size.

Lotus used the occasion to raise other issues, too. The SCCA previously had nixed such Lotus refinements as oil coolers, magnesium wheels and rear disc brakes. But, they allowed up to six Weber carburetors on the Ferrari 250. On a Wednesday, Chapman requested a hearing at the next meeting of the SCCA Car Classification Committee. The reply came on the following Monday. The meeting had been held over the weekend. The Super Seven 1500 was out because the car was too fast to race. Period. Case closed. Some years later the Club changed their mind and accepted the 1500 engine, but Chapman had to wait until Tom Robertson's 1977 victory to enjoy the last laugh.

Bob Bent takes a victory lap at Cotati in 1963. The 1963 season was an all-out effort for Bent, culminating in a Pacific Coast Class F Production Championship and a Zippo lighter from Lotus.

Bob Bent: Still Got That Zippo

Hundreds of Seven-owners assaulted the SCCA circuits in the 1960's. The typical specimen resembled Bob Bent. Bent started racing a Corvette in 1957, progressed through a Sebring Sprite, a Formula Jr. and an Austin Healey. It was all good fun—he scored a few wins, but

Anatoly Aruntunoff pedals by in his indomitable Series 2 Seven at IRP in 1962. The Seven, outfitted with $8.00 recaps on original casings, finished second to an Alfa.

Old Sevens Never Die

Anatoly Aruntunoff is an American motorsportsman who indulges himself with all manner of cars, just for fun. He owns his own race course, collects early Cooper race cars, drives anything from Abarths to Pegasos in Historic car races and competes regularly with a Morgan in the SCCA. He is also a Seven enthusiast.

Aruntunoff acquired his Series 2 Seven A America for the SCCA G Production in 1961. He broke the car in with a 1600-mile drive from Los Angeles to his home base in Oklahoma. The car was campaigned for two seasons and Aruntunoff won a class trophy in all but one race. In that one, two of the three cars that beat him were disqualified for illegal modifications. The engine was nothing short of remarkable: "One time my car and another Seven lost the front exhaust manifold nut simultaneously, and the resulting heat boiled our radiators dry. The other fellow pulled in, but I, with a crankcase full of Multigrade Phillips Trop-Arctic, STP and Wynn's Special Additive For Foreign Cars, kept going. I finished third, with all the paint burned off the cylinder head and valve springs that floated the valves over 3700 rpm. The engine maintained 20 pounds of oil pressure and neither the bearings nor the cylinder walls were marked. It was probably the best little BMC unit ever built!"

In 1962, Aruntunoff was towing the Seven home from a meet when the trailer hitch broke. His rig shot into the oncoming lane and hit a Chevrolet head on. No one was injured, but the Seven was a proper mess. The car was rebuilt and sold to Allan Girdler, who at the time was editor of *Road & Track*.

Girdler raced the car for several more seasons and drove it on the street. One day he spun the Seven into the path of a truck. Girdler was critically injured but recovered and rebuilt the car. He retired from competition after another couple of seasons and the Series 2 Seven A America went off to a new home.

Aruntunoff managed to keep tabs on his old Seven. To this day he follows the car's progress in SCCA events. Oh yes, there was another crash—a "somewhat comprehensive" one—but the Seven was put together again and sent out for more. What a trooper!

nothing dramatic. In 1961, he decided to buy a winner. His Lotus
Seven A America arrived in kit form near the end of the year. The
pieces fell into place just like the manual said, but there was one surprise: someone at Cheshunt had filled the gearbox with water. Bent
used the strip-down as an excuse to install the close ratio gears. The
only other modification was an American-made anti-roll bar. He'd
heard the English ones broke.

The first outing was in April 1962, at Stockton, California. The engine
had all the Sprite options, but the car ran stock 3½-inch rims with
Michelin X tires. The first thing Bent discovered was that his competitors
used either the optional Lotus 5-inch wheels or 4½-inch cheaters from
the Spitfire. Then he realized that his tires were useless, no matter how
wide. For his second race, Bent fitted the latest Goodyear Bluestreaks on
wider wheels and scored a seventh place. He improved with every race
until, by season's end, he was fourth overall in the Pacific Coast Division.

Bent's only DNF that season was at Santa Barbara. He was gaining
on the leader in the inside of a corner, when the driver of the Alfa
looked over, turned his wheel and shoved the Lotus into the hay bales.
The Alfa driver was suspended, but Bent's Seven was a pretzel.

The chassis was rebuilt that winter. Bent gave the engine a Huffacker
cam and some head work, which raised compression to 12.5 to 1. An
overbore to 0.030 brought displacement to 970 cc's and an estimated
power output of 75 brake. The 1963 season was to be an all out effort.

Bent ran six races. He scored two firsts at Cotati, one each at Kent
and Newport and seconds at Salt Lake and Candlestick Park. The

Bent at Candlestick Park SCCA race in September 1963.

63

season ended with a gearbox that jumped out of 4th gear and a Pacific Coast Class F Production Championship. Lotus sent the champ a letter of commendation and a $2.50 Zippo lighter to mark the achievement. By 1964, the Triumph Spitfire had come into its own in F Production and the Seven was no longer competitive. Bent sold the car. He briefly raced an AC Bristol but business demands caught up with him and he retired from the circuit.

Ten years passed and then Bent saw his first historic car race. The old juices started flowing again. He knew the whereabouts of his old Seven, but the owner wouldn't sell. The car had survived auto-crossing from 1970 to 1975 and was in fine condition. Bent talked the owner into letting him drive the Seven in the 1977 Laguna Seca historic Races in Monterey, California.

During practice, the car felt just the same. It might have been 1963 all over again. The gearbox still jumped out of 4th, but only on Turn 3 (a hundred mile an hour corner for the Seven). On the first lap, Bent had moved up a couple of places when the lever leapt out of gear on the turn. He pushed it home but it jumped out again and the car veered off the track. Fearful of overturning if he spun the car, Bent braced himself for the impending meeting with the Armco. The Lotus was destroyed. Bent suffered a concussion and five fractured ribs. That was the end of the Seven, but not the story. Bent brought a Lotus Elite to the historic scene in 1978 and 1979. He's looking for even more fun in the 80's.

Tom Robertson vs. British Leyland: No Contest

The 1977 SCCA Championship runoffs were held at the Road Atlanta Track in Georgia. The Triumph TR 7 had been developed into a dominant Class D Production car with the help of tremendous factory support. British Leyland wanted the championship. There was little spectator interest because the race was sure to be a walkover. The only question was whether Lee Mueller or Ken Slagle would get to the finish line first.

In the fourth lap a 1963 blue Lotus Super Seven appeared in fifth

Cool and collected Tom Robertson gets everything ready.

Robertson takes Super Seven for a victory lap. He added front
spoiler to neutralize the lift generated by clam shells.

place, and gaining. Tom Robertson was at the helm. One by one, the
leaders fell to the Seven's superior braking and acceleration. By the
eighth lap, the savy Robertson had caught Slagle and the crowd of
25,000 came alive. The Seven began its precise maneuvers, looking for a
way around. Robertson found the weakness, outbraked Slagle in a corner, got inside and was away.

Mueller had three seconds in hand, but Robertson was closing by a
second a lap. By the 11th circuit, the Seven was in the Triumph's draft.
Robertson slipped past on the inside. "We were going about 115 miles
an hour and we had to slow to 95 or 100 for the curve. The TR was a
much heavier car and had to brake earlier, so I took advantage of that.
I went under him, he saw me, moved over and hit me in the left rear
by the wheel." Robertson held his line, got by, and went on to win by
six seconds. A 14-year-old Lotus Seven had won the SCCA National
Championship over the best British Leyland had to offer. Chapman must
have roared. (See Chapter 11 review of Robertson's race preparation.)

The French Connection

In 1964, G. J. (Jabby) Crombac, Lotus enthusiast, Seven-owner and editor of the French magazine *Sport Auto*, promoted a competition. Ford of France purchased twenty Series 2 kits for what was called "Operation Ford Jeunesse." Contestants were French motorsport clubs.

In the first phase of competition, the kits were given to the youngest members of each club for assembly. The youngsters decorated the car with the crest of their province and set the Seven up for club racing. In the second phase, each province nominated its most promising driver who would race the car for one season. Club members took care of all maintenance and preparation.

Operation Ford Jeunesse was a tremendous success, gaining fine publicity for *Sport Auto* and Ford of France. The racing was closely competitive and the Sevens gave French race goers a very exciting season. Among the extremely talented drivers who raced Sevens that year were Patrick Depailler, Henri Pescarolo, and Johnny Servoz-Gavin. Depailler would of course become a familiar name in Formula I.

Australia: The Clubman

Clubman racing in Australia paralleled the same class in England. By the mid 1950's, the circuit attracted a large following. There were few regulations. The cars had to be open two-seaters of less than 1½-liter engine capacity. They could be one-offs or series-produced, but had to conform to the "Clubman spirit" which meant fenders and bodywork. While there weren't supposed to be exotic engines, just about any modification of a mass-produced motor was allowed.

At first the Clubman Class was rather casual. The grids were mixtures of production cars, specials and factory sports racers like the Lotus Eleven and Lola. The Lotus Seven began to change all that. A few Series 1's had found their way to Australia and, inevitably, onto the race tracks. The car looked right and performed even better.

A turning point came in 1962 when the Super Seven 109E came on the scene. Fast and easy to handle, the Super Seven was tailor-made for Clubman. Also, the car was recognizable—the Super Seven had an identity. Best of all, the kit was relatively inexpensive. Before long, most starting grids were filled with this car. The Clubman Class belonged to the Lotus Seven.

The early sixties was a growth period in Australian motorsport. Import licensing and tariffs were suspended, and customers were eager to try the latest British sports cars on the new tracks that were built. Racing classes were more rigidly defined, and the Seven provided the definition for Clubman.

Demon Mods

In the 1962 and 1963 seasons most 109E Cosworths were raced as delivered. Nothing is stagnant in racing, however, and the demon mods began to appear. Larger valves, higher compression and all manner of cam shafts were tried. When the 116E 1500's arrived, common practice was to bore the 109E to 1475 cc's to remain competitive. Finally, Garrie Cooper of Elfin Racing decided to do the Lotus one better and build his own type Seven car. The Elfin Clubman was Cosworth-powered, too, but generally better finished than its near-twin (see Chapter 10). Soon after the Elfin came the NOTA Sportsman with an all-alloy body, swing axle at the front and a distinct Lotus Seven look. So far little had been done to improve on the original.

By 1963 most race meetings ran Clubman with regular production

The car in front is the Seven-like NOTA Sportsman, driven by Siman Lee in 1967 Australian Clubman meet. The inspiration is right behind.

classes. This delighted the Seven-owners, but dismayed the drivers of MGA's, Healeys, Sprites and the like. That year Ian Geoghegan and Arnold Ahrenfeld, both in Super Sevens, finished first and second in the New South Wales Production Sports Car Championships. The following year, the New South Wales Lotus dealer, Geoghegan Motors, sponsored a five-race series for the Clubman. Bob Beasley won in a Seven, but the competition brought out a surprising number of Elfins, NOTA's and other one-off Seven imitators. A crisis loomed when the Australian competition ruling body (CAMS) announced that, beginning in 1965, the Clubman Class would be limited to 1100 cc's! The aim was to slow the escalating cost of racing by concentrating on the variety of mass-produced 1-liter engines available from England and Japan.

New South Wales dutifully ignored the edict and stuck to the 1500-cc maximum capacity. (They did include provision for 1100 Clubmans and drew quite a few.) The circuit was still dominated by 116E Sevens, but the cars began to utilize new technology. Four-wheel disc brakes appeared along with 6-inch-wide alloy wheels. Other modifications included chassis stiffening, dual front wishbones and separate anti-roll bars. The basic design had become long in the tooth.

For the next few years Clubman racing continued without much change. Other drivers entered the scene, including Alex MacArthur, who won the NSW Series in 1966 and 1967, Syd Howard in a very modernized Super Seven, Bill March in a 1-liter car and Lorraine Hill, who was the prettiest Seven driver of all.

It's Bill March (in front) and
Arnold Ahrenfeld at June 1964 RAC
Trophy Race. *Photo: Ian Elliott*

In the early sixties the
Clubman class in Australia
simply belonged to the Seven.

Bob Beasley on the Clubman circuit.

Hustler

The 1100-cc Class became more popular for the very reason initially cited by CAMS (a farsighted rules body?) and encouraged the one-off special builder. Eventually, a fellow by the name of Tony Simmonds sat down and studied the rules with the idea of building not another Seven replica, but a state-of-the-art Clubman. In 1968 he produced the Hustler. An all out racing car, the Hustler had adjustable suspension, 8-inch-wide wheels and absolute minimum ground clearance. The car was so low and squat the fenders towered above the body.

The Super Sevens competed gamely with the young upstarts. There weren't many firsts or seconds, but in sheer numbers at least, the Seven continued to dominate the field. Outside the province of New South Wales, the Clubman class raced the production cars and remained competitive until the early 70's. Owners were required to fit rigid doors and comply with other foolishness, but the Seven adapted more easily than competitors to the wide, low-profile tires.

The Clubman is alive and well even today. The car that brought life and longevity to the class is still around as well. The Seven's been chopped and channeled, the wheels are as wide as the body, the driver can adjust the carbs from the cockpit; but the space frame chassis came from Cheshunt.

John Morton leads Ronnie Bucknum' MGB at Dodger Stadium in Decembe 1963 race. *Photos: Dave Friedma*

70

Seven cornering techniques as demonstrated at Santa Barbara Raceway (California) in May 1962.

5 The Se

Marketed only eight months, the Lotus-built
Series 3 twin-cam remains alive today in
Caterham guise as the all-time favorite.
Photo: Bill Motta

s 3: Enduring Classic

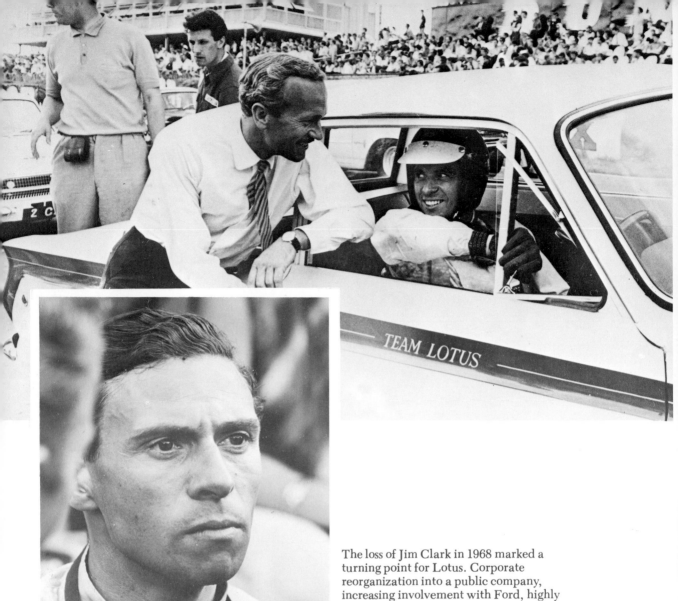

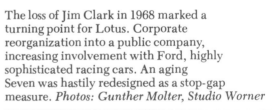

The loss of Jim Clark in 1968 marked a
turning point for Lotus. Corporate
reorganization into a public company,
increasing involvement with Ford, highly
sophisticated racing cars. An aging
Seven was hastily redesigned as a stop-gap
measure. *Photos: Gunther Molter, Studio Worner*

For Lotus and for every enthusiast who followed Formula 1 racing, 1968 was edged in black. Jim Clark's death at Hockenheim had come only three months after his record-breaking 25th Grand Prix victory. Chapman ordered new bonnet badges of black and silver to commemorate Clark's contribution to Team Lotus and to the sport, and the familiar green and yellow emblems were retired for one year. Of course, Formula 1 went on. Graham Hill moved up to become number one driver and won his second World Championship, bringing home a third Constructor's Title for Lotus in the process.

Lotus was reorganized that year to turn Lotus Cars Ltd. into a public holding company. Shares were duly issued, but the only stockholders were Colin Chapman and Peter Kirwan-Taylor. New groups were formed, including Lotus Cars (Service), Lotus Cars (Sales) and Lotus Components. Team Lotus split off to become a separate company with their own shops and personnel, but still headed by Chapman.

Lotus Components inherited the Seven. This group had shown financial losses for several years and desperately needed a rapid turn-around. Mike Warner, who had left Lotus the previous year to start his own company, came back to take charge. He looked over the 1968 Ford offerings and immediately decided to build a Series 3 Seven with the new Cortina 1600-cc crossflow engine. He felt this could be a money-maker and wanted to get it to market fast. The official announcement came in September.

Going With What They Had

Lotus was well aware of the chassis failures on the Series 2 and intended to correct them on the Series 3. Unfortunately, Lotus Components was under the gun to reverse their losses and had to expedite plans for the new car. There wasn't time to redesign, and the first Series 3 chassis was nearly identical to the Series 2.

There was some justification for the decision to go with what they had. The Series 3 was known to be an interim model. "Fun cars" (dune buggies and Seven imitators) had stormed the marketplace and Lotus designers were already working on a Seven for the seventies. The Series 4 would be radically different in appearance, with a completely new chassis underneath. Why change now?

Then too, the Seven was no longer competitive, if allowed at all, in modern racing, so there wouldn't be the opportunity to overstress the chassis. So went the theory. In fact, one didn't buy a Seven to potter around in, and high performance motoring was enough to bring out all of the old weaknesses.

As production got rolling, a few minor chassis modifications were incorporated. The exhaust system bracketry was revised to accept a new muffler and shroud, and the exhaust pipe now curved under the axle to exit at the rear. No more scorched ankles. The Series 3 was the first Seven to fit seat belt mounts, although of dubious value. The outboard fixtures were solid enough, being welded to the chassis tube. The inboard fittings were merely attached to the alloy undertray, which flexed alarmingly when the belts were cinched up tight. A new roll-over bar was offered, too, but also was more cosmetic than functional. The primary hoop mounted ineffectually to the tops of the shock absorbers.

The works did strengthen the chassis late in Series 3 production when the Super Seven came on the market. While not extensive, the modifications were a big step in the right direction. The rear trailing arm chassis mount was reinforced with a tube that met the mounting point and ran forward to the lower chassis rail. Additional tubes triangulated the bottom engine bay. A diagonal was also added to each side of the chassis below the scuttle. The new tubes significantly increased the rigidity of the forward part of the chassis. The chassis still wasn't perfect, but it was a partial return to the strength of the old Mark 6. Additional modifications are suggested in Chapter 12.

Built as an interim model while the Series 4 was readied for production, the Series 3 shows little change from the 2. One distinct difference is new muffler and shroud, with an extended exhaust pipe exiting at the rear. Note also the slightly sharper radius to rear fender, side reflector addition and optional Brand Lotus alloy wheels. Rear quarter windows were added to the top with the Series 2 Super Seven 1500 in 1962, but disappeared with the Series 4.
Photo: Bill Motta

Boulevard Racer

In appearance, the Series 3 differed only slightly from the Series 2. A new rear axle gave the car a wider track and the rear fenders were extended accordingly. A sharper radius to the fender also distinguished the car from earlier Sevens. For some reason, Lotus did not alter the front fenders to cover the new track or wider tires, so the front took on a "boulevard racer" look.

The new crossflow engine used a downdraft carburetor that necessitated a bulge *cum* air scoop on the right side of the bonnet top. When the twin-cam was fitted late in production, louvers were added to the rear of the bonnet to assist under-hood ventilation. Otherwise, the body was identical with the Series 2 Seven and, as a result, interchangeable. The front fenders still carried running lights, but separate amber turn indicators were placed underneath the headlights. The Lucas taillights were used until the twin-cam version, when rectangular Britax units were substituted. The gas tank capacity was increased to eight gallons and the filler moved to the rear body panel.

The dash panel took on a completely new look with this car. The ignition switch on left-hand drive cars was moved from the center of the dash to the extreme right-hand corner. A fuel gauge appeared for the first time. And, the old toggle switches were traded for rockers labeled with symbols. Other instruments on the dash included speedometer, tachometer and gauges for oil pressure and water temperature.

New amber turn indicator can be seen below headlight. Running light is mounted on fender as on previous series. Except for new hub and raised steering rack, front suspension was unchanged.
Photo: Dennis Ortenburger

There was also a new 14-inch black polyvinylchloride (PVC) steering wheel. (Several cars, though, were delivered with leather rims.) The upholstery, dash covering and carpets were standardized in black. The seats were covered with a new perforated vinyl and treated to slightly more padding. So this was the new Seven: a little nicer, but still recognizable to the enthusiast.

Slight padding and perforated vinyl upholstery made the Series 3 interior a little nicer, but shiny alloy tranny tunnel is still exposed. *Photo: Dennis Ortenburger*

Lotus Gets The Message

Lotus finally took notice of the anguished cries directed at the Standard (Triumph) 10 rear axle. The Series 3 sported one from the Ford Escort. The Escort axle seemed to have everything: robust construction of half-shafts and case, wider track, good selection of differential ratios and, oh dear, a different bolt circle. Series 2 owners couldn't retrofit unless they bought new wheels, too. In keeping with the trend toward wider and lower-profile tires, the Series 3 came with 13-inch wheels on 5½-inch rims. Standard specification was the Escort steel wheel with Brand Lotus alloy rims optional. Brakes were still drums, but 8-inches diameter by 1½-inches wide. The rear suspension was otherwise identical with the Series 2.

The front suspension used a new hub to correspond with the change in bolt circle from 3¾ to 4¼ inches. Curiously, the hub came from a British Leyland subsidiary and not Ford. Nine-inch disc brakes were standard, the front drums going the way of the TR axle. A-arms, sway bar, springs and shocks were the same as on the Series 2.

The only significant change in the front suspension came in a relocation of the steering rack late in Series 3 production. The Series 2 had shown a pronounced upward angle of the steering arms in steady state. The angle increased during cornering and braking attitudes. The result was a toe-in condition and a considerable amount of bump steer. Lotus raised the rack by about 1½ inches to bring the steering arms nearly parallel to the ground. This virtually eliminated the error in geometry and made the Seven a more stable car, especially with the new generation tires.

Enthusiasts Get Their Engine

Series 3 buyers initially had a choice of two engines. Both were based on the new Ford 225E. The "economy" engine was the crossflow

Brand Lotus alloy wheels were optional.

No, this is not a Series 3, but Bill Wade's restored Series 2 provides excellent illustration of the corrected steering rack position. Steering arms are now parallel to ground.
Photo: Owen Wuillemin

pushrod 1300-cc unit from the Escort GT. This engine was rated at a healthy 68 bhp and gave excellent fuel economy.

The standard engine was the Cortina 1600-cc crossflow. This exceptionally efficient motor was rated at 84 bhp at 5800 rpm. Equipped with a 4-branch exhaust manifold and a twin choke Weber downdraft type 32 DFM, the Cortina was box stock with no Lotus modifications whatsoever. The engine was smooth, willing and grossly underrated. With the optional 3.7 differential (standard was the 4.125) the Series 3 crossflow was as fast as the old 1500 Cosworth. Lotus retained the faultless 116E gearbox.

The Super Seven model was announced only eight months before the end of the series. Early factory notices had said the Series 3 could not accommodate the new Lotus twin cam engine. They were wrong. The Super Seven (Lotus Seven SS) carried the 1600-cc twin-cam Elan engine at 90 bhp. Most Super Sevens, though, were ordered Holbay-tuned. The Lotus-Holbay twin-cam was claimed to produce 125 horses at 6200 rpm and 116 pounds of torque at 4500 rpm. The engine used dual Weber 40-DCOE's, as in the Elan, but with a free flow 4-branch exhaust. The compression ratio remained 9.5 to 1. The increased performance came from port and combustion chamber detailing, higher lift cams, and the exhaust system. In truth, the horsepower rating was probably optimistic. But the Lotus-Holbay twin-cam was without temperment, extremely flexible, and the engine Seven enthusiasts wanted.

Lotus offered one other version of the Series 3: a Holbay-modified 1600-cc crossflow. This engine was only fitted to the Seven S, which was a different creature altogether (see Chapter 9).

Turning Fun Into Contraband

Mike Warner asked Lotus Sales to help design a marketing campaign to take advantage of the "fun car" movement. Although the fun-car fad was initiated by the VW-based dune buggy, a number of Lotus Seven imitators had appeared on the scene. Series 3 advertising sought to remind everyone just who invented fun motoring.

SEVEN · LOTUS · SERIES 3 ✳

SOLE DISTRIBUTOR - *CATERHAM CAR SALES* =

Caterham Car Sales, sole U.K. Seven distributor, had no trouble selling both kits and fully-assembled cars. Kit prices were £775 ($1860 at an exchange rate of $2.40 per pound) for the 1600 and £1250 ($3000) for the Holbay twin-cam. Both cars could also be purchased factory direct.

Marketing was, however, a moot point in America. The Series 3 was never completely Federalized to conform with 1968 U.S. emission and safety regulations. The car was technically illegal. Like a lot of contraband, that alone made the new Seven immensely desirable. Nothing spurred Yankee ingenuity like the challenge of bringing a Series 3 into the States. Fake chassis plates, kits sent in three or four parcels marked "spare auto parts," cars registered as dune buggies or home builts—all were tried with varying degrees of success.

In April 1970 the Series 3 ceased production with approximately 350 cars built. The line didn't die, however. Manufacture continues to this day under the banner of Caterham Cars. (See Chapter 7.)

Caterham Car Sales was the sole U.K. distributor for the Series 3, and issued the sales brochure reproduced here. For more on Caterham see Chapter 7.

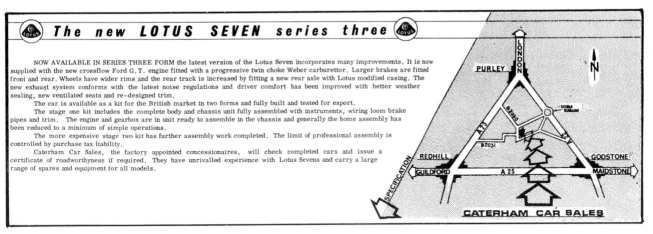

The new LOTUS SEVEN series three

NOW AVAILABLE IN SERIES THREE FORM the latest version of the Lotus Seven incorporates many improvements. It is now supplied with the new crossflow Ford G.T. engine fitted with a progressive twin choke Weber carburettor. Larger brakes are fitted front and rear. Wheels have wider rims and the rear track is increased by fitting a new rear axle with Lotus modified casing. The new exhaust system conforms with the latest noise regulations and driver comfort has been improved with better weather sealing, new ventilated seats and re-designed trim.

The car is available as a kit for the British market in two forms and fully built and tested for export.

The stage one kit includes the complete body and chassis unit fully assembled with instruments, wiring loom brake pipes and trim. The engine and gearbox are in unit ready to assemble in the chassis and generally the home assembly has been reduced to a minimum of simple operations.

The more expensive stage two kit has further assembly work completed. The limit of professional assembly is controlled by purchase tax liability.

Caterham Car Sales, the factory appointed concessionaires, will check completed cars and issue a certificate of roadworthyness if required. They have unrivalled experience with Lotus Sevens and carry a large range of spares and equipment for all models.

SPECIFICATION

CHASSIS – Tubular space frame.

BODY – Aluminium alloy stressed panels with self-coloured glass fibre wings, nose cowl and carburettor air intake.

ENGINE – Ford 2250E. 1300c.c. or 1600c.c. G.T. cross flow unit with twin choke Weber carburettor.

GEARBOX – Ford. Remote gear change with synchromesh on all four forward gears.

REAR AXLE – Ford with modified Lotus casing. 4·12 : 1 ratio for 1300c.c. engine, 3·77 : 1 ratio for 1600c.c. engine.

FRONT SUSPENSION – Wide based tubular lower wishbone and forged top link located by anti-roll bar. Combined coil spring and damper units are used.

REAR SUSPENSION – Well located live rear axle controlled by trailing links and 'A' frame. Combined spring and damper units are used.

STEERING – Rack and pinion. An alloy spoked steering wheel with waterproof P.V.C. rim is fitted.

INTERIOR TRIM – Black pile carpets with matching weatherproof trim. Seats are covered in black ventilated P.V.C.

WEATHER EQUIPMENT – Sidescreens and black weatherproof hood incorporating large rear view panel. Hood folds into boot under a waterproof cover when not in use. Twin windscreen wipers are fitted. Improved body sealing is now incorporated.

FUEL SYSTEM – 8 gallon tank with filler in rear body panel.

BRAKES – Hydraulic. Disc front and drum rear with 'fly off' action handbrake to rear units.

COOLING – Pressurised system with automatic, temperature controlled electric cooling fan with manual overrider switch.

ELECTRICAL – 12 volt negative earth system with 39 amp. hour battery. Double dipping headlamps with separate sidelamps and direction indicators. Stop and tail lamps and number plate illumination at rear.

INSTRUMENTS – Electric tachometer. Speedometer with mileage recorder. Ammeter. Fuel contents. Combined oil pressure and water temperature gauge. Flick switches control lights, horn, indicators and wipers.

WHEELS – 13 inch diameter with 5½ J rims fitted with high speed tyres. Spare wheel is mounted externally at rear of car.

EXHAUST SYSTEM – High efficiency system with large capacity absorption type silencer and tailpipe to rear of car.

NOTE – Due to continuous development this specification may alter at any time without notice.

OPTIONAL EXTRAS

LIMITED SLIP DIFFERENTIAL UNIT	ROLL OVER BAR
FOUR BRANCH EXHAUST DOWNPIPE	SEAT BELTS
CLOSE RATIO GEARBOX	OIL COOLER
ENGINE TUNING EQUIPMENT	TONNEAU COVER
SPECIAL WHEELS	HEATER

MANY SERIES THREE PARTS CAN BE FITTED TO EARLIER CARS. CATERHAM CAR SALES WILL BE PLEASED TO ADVISE OWNERS WISHING TO IMPROVE THEIR LOTUS SEVEN PARTS ARE AVAILABLE FROM THE STORES DEPARTMENT. TELEPHONE CATERHAM 42381.

* L O T U S * S E V E N * S E R I E S * T H R E E * * *

Just For The Record . . .

A tradition at Norwich was a yearly Lotus open house. The public was invited to tour the works, picnic and enjoy the countryside. One of the attractions was the assembly of a Seven kit. The 1969 outing saw the all-time record established. John Robinson of Lotus Components put together a Series 3 Seven in 4 hours, 35 minutes and 5 seconds! To prove there was no sleight of hand, Graham Nearn took the car out for a test spin on the works's circuit. To everyone's surprise, nothing fell off.

Breathtaking Performance

The Series 3 benefited from the wider track and standard 5½-inch rims. Cornering power bordered on the fantastic unless, as with the earlier cars, the road surface was wet or bumpy. The Seven was still an understeerer, but the available power made for easy correction.

The economy model with 1300-cc Escort engine had a top speed of about 100 miles per hour, and the car could do 0 to 60 in eight plus a fraction seconds. Fuel economy was excellent at approximately 30 mpg. The Seven had taken on some weight by this time—both crossflow versions tipped the scales at 1204 pounds.

The 1600 crossflow performed almost identically with the old 1500 Cosworth, a measure of just how nice this box stock motor was. Top speed was 103, and 0 to 60 times in the high sevens. The engine still gave a respectable 25 miles per gallon.

The Super Seven with the Ford twin-cam gave a truly breathtaking experience. With the Holbay option the car would do 0 to 60 in a fraction under seven seconds and top out at 103 mph. The twin-cam Super Seven was the quickest ever, but barely. While hardly overweight at 1260 pounds, the car weighed almost 200 pounds more than the 1500. That made all the difference. Stop watches aside, everyone who tested the car considered the twin-cam the most exciting Seven of all. Fuel economy was around 20 mpg which also make it the thirstiest. No matter. When polls are taken, the Seven Series 3 twin-cam always comes out number one.

The old criticisms were still valid, twin-cam or no. The seats were non-adjustable and interior dimensions favored the slender. Getting in with the top up was an event that should be recorded on film. The headlights vibrated at speed, making night driving a psychedelic adventure. The car was still as rough riding as a cob. If that weren't enough, the new exhaust system produced an odd hiss, like the mating call of a passionate snake. All these shortcomings melted away the moment you accelerated down a winding road on a summer's day. Seven motoring was for fun. Nothing else really mattered.

Road & Track borrowed an illegally-imported Super Seven Twin-Cam to conduct this 1973 road test. U.S. government officials read every word and subsequently confiscated the car.

PRICE

List price (England).........$3502
Price as tested, Denver, Colo.$5450

IMPORTER

Not imported for resale (see text)

ENGINE

Type.....Lotus-Ford dohc inline 4
Bore x stroke, mm.....82.6 x 72.8
Equivalent in........3.25 x 2.86
Displacement, cc/cu in..1558/95.2
Compression ratio...........9.5:1
Bhp @ rpm...........125 @ 6200
Equivalent mph..............107
Torque @ rpm......116 @ 4500
Equivalent mph..............78
Carburetion....two Weber 40 DCOE
Type fuel required.......premium
Emission control........PCV valve

DRIVE TRAIN

Transmission......4-spd. manual
Gear ratios: 4th (1.00).....3.90:1
3rd (1.40)..............5.46:1
2nd (2.01)..............7.84:1
1st (2.97).............11.58:1
Final drive ratio..........3.90:1

CHASSIS & BODY

Layout.....front engine/rear drive
Body/frame: space-type frame of
steel tubing and stressed alumi-
num panels: fiberglass fenders
and nose cowling
Brake type: front, 9-in. disc; rear,
8 x 1.5-in. drum
Swept area, sq in........225.4
Wheels...........alloy 5.5J x 13
Tires...........Dunlop 165 HR 13
Steering type......rack & pinion
Turns, lock-to-lock.........2.7
Turning circle, ft........29.6
Front suspension: lower A-arm and
single link, coil springs, tube
shocks, anti-roll bar
Rear suspension: live axle with
trailing arms and A-brackets, coil
springs, tube shocks

ACCOMMODATION

Seating capacity, persons......2
Seat width.............2 x 18.0
Head room.................34.0
Seat back adjustment, degrees...0
Driver comfort rating (scale of 100):
See text

INSTRUMENTATION

Instruments: speedometer, tachometer, water temperature, oil
pressure, ammeter
Warning lights: directionals, high
beam

MAINTENANCE

Service intervals, mi
Oil change...............6000
Filter change............6000
Chassis lube.............1500
Minor tuneup.........as needed
Major tuneup.........as needed
Warranty, mo/mi...........none

GENERAL

Curb weight, lb............1210
Test weight................1520
Weight distribution (with
driver), front/rear, %....50/50
Wheelbase, in..............89.0
Track, front/rear......49.0/52.0
Overall length............133.0
Width..................61.0
Height.................37.0
Ground clearance............3.0
Overhang, front/rear......18/26
Usable trunk space, cu ft..see text
Fuel tank capacity, U.S. gal....9.6

CALCULATED DATA

Lb/bhp (test weight)........12.2
Mph/1000 rpm (4th gear).....17.3
Engine revs/mi (60 mph)....3470
Engine speed @ 70 mph.....4050
Piston travel, ft/mi........1055
Cu ft/ton mi..............166
R&T wear index..............58
R&T steering index.........0.80
Brake swept area sq in/ton.332

ROAD TEST RESULTS

ACCELERATION

Time to distance, sec:
0–100 ft..................2.8
0–250 ft..................5.2
0–500 ft..................8.3
0–750 ft.................10.9
0–1000 ft................13.2
0–1320 ft (¼ mi)........15.7
Speed at end of ¼ mi, mph....80
Time to speed, sec:
0–30 mph.................2.7
0–40 mph.................3.9
0–50 mph.................5.6
0–60 mph.................7.7
0–70 mph................10.5
0–80 mph................15.6
Passing exposure time, sec:
To pass car going 50 mph....5.7

FUEL CONSUMPTION

Normal driving, mpg..........20
Cruising range, mi...........192

SPEEDS IN GEARS

4th gear (5500 rpm)..........96
3rd (6200)................79
2nd (6200)................54
1st (6200)................36

BRAKES

Panic stop from 80 mph:
Max. deceleration rate, % g..75
Control.................good
Pedal effort for 50%-g stop, lb..55
Fade test: percent increase in pedal
effort to maintain 50%-g deceler-
ation rate in 6 stops from 60
mph...................10
Parking: Hold 30% grade?......no
Overall brake rating.....very good

SPEEDOMETER ERROR

30 mph indicated is actually...32.5
40 mph.....................43.0
60 mph.....................63.7
70 mph.....................74.1
80 mph.....................85.5
Odometer, 10.0 mi......not taken

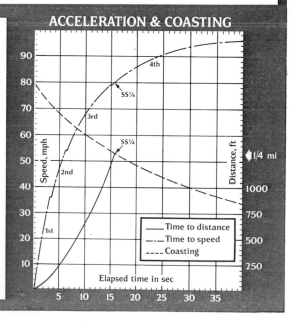

ACCELERATION & COASTING

Speed, mph / Distance, ft

4th
SS¼
3rd
SS¼
2nd
1st
¼ mi
1000
750
500
250

Elapsed time in sec

—— Time to distance
—·—· Time to speed
----- Coasting

6

Clam shell fenders make the Series 4 unmistakably a Seven, but traditionalists didn't care for the slick, fresh from the mold look of everything else.
Photo: Lotus Press Office

Series 4: A Totally Different Seven

The Lotus Seven Series 4 was born into a time of trouble. Although Lotus had won their fourth Formula I Championship, Team Lotus number one driver Jochen Rindt was killed at Monza practicing for the Italian Grand Prix. The fiscal columns were in the red again. By 1971, both Lotus Components and Lotus Racing had closed their shops for good. The Elan Sprint was introduced to mixed reviews. With the new "Big-Valve" twin-cam engine, the Sprint was the fastest Elan yet, but the detailing belied the ten-year development effort. The price of all Lotus road cars was up. Unsold vehicles lined the runways at Hethel.

Chapman's designers were at work on the Series 4 before the Series 3 had even reached the marketplace. Lotus Components reportedly had £30,000 of development money to play with. The initial design parameters were laid down to achieve two goals. The first was to take advantage of the dune buggy/fun car boom. The second was to regain the competitive image of the old Series 2. A new racing class had been devised in England. The *Formula F100* recalled the Clubman concept of relatively inexpensive, competitive racing. The Formula F100 was to be for sports cars what Formula Ford was to open wheelers. In fact, Lotus toyed with the idea of modifying their Type 61 Formula Ford into a two-seater fourth generation Lotus Seven. A mid-engined Seven sounded exciting but F100 rules specified an all-enveloping body while the beach buggy/fun car image demanded open fenders.

What to do? Lotus opted to scratch goal number two and aim specifically at the non-sporting market. In keeping with the new Lotus image, the new Seven was to be more a proper automobile and less a rough-shod race car with license plates. A completely re-styled body would be designed to fit a separate chassis. A new type number was even assigned: the Series 4 Seven was actually designated as a Lotus 60.

The net result of all these decisions was—a flop. The Series 4 managed in one stroke to alienate the Seven cult without finding a stable place for itself in the fickle youth market. The car was a misfit. Initial sales were brisk enough as Lotus rode the fun car wave, but when the surf subsided, enthusiasts demanded a return of the Series 3 and the youth market kept hacking up Volkswagens.

Radical redesign by Peter Lucas resulted in an all-fiberglass body bolted to separate tube and steel chassis. *Drawing: Tony Divey*

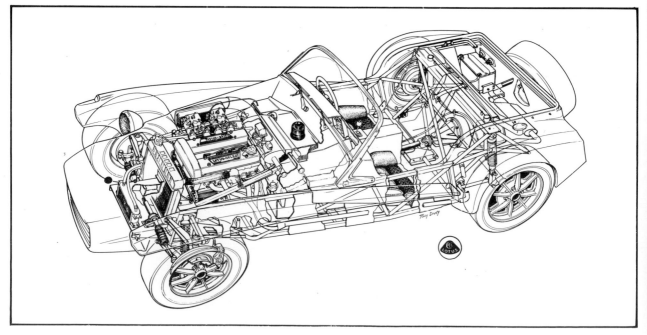

Return Of The Ladder

The Series 4 chassis was the work of designer Peter Lucas. The design criteria of a separate body and frame dictated a shift from the traditional Seven space frame toward the conventional ladder. The stressed undertray and rear panel disappeared. Lucas used sheet steel to replace the alloy paneling on the sides of the chassis and to form the front suspension bay and scuttle.

The rear of the chassis was made of round and square section tubing and sheet steel. New bracketry picked up the revised suspension. The chassis was slightly longer and wider than earlier Sevens, which gave a welcome increase in interior space. With the body bolted in place, the whole thing seemed rigid enough for street use which, after all, was the car's purpose. Any form of competition revealed some flexibility in the back end, but most of the old suspension pickup problems were finally cured. Exceptions were the chassis pickups for the lower arms which were prone to cracking. As might be expected, the separate body and chassis gave rise to groans and rattles unfamiliar to the classic-Seven enthusiast. Owners quickly developed chassis modifications to surmount these minor irritations. (See Chapter 12.)

An Easy-Clean Surface

The Series 4 body was a soft-edged version of its predecessors. The polished fiberglass shell looked like a come-on for a harried housewife: no hard-to-reach cracks or crevices and an easy-clean surface, like a molded bathtub. The front wings reached back to meet the rear fenders

The smooth fiberglass body was appropriate for the Tupperware Age, but satisfied no-one. Note extended front fender and elongated rear; slight lip on boxy cowl.
Photo: Stewart White

Series 4 bonnet hinges at front like Jag XKE and balances in open position. Dr. Casey Rasilewicz has added Cromodora alloy wheels to his car. *Photo: Dennis Ortenburger*

in a long, uninterrupted sweep. The cowl grew an upper lip that strained toward the ground. The rear fenders stretched backwards nearly a foot to become more egg-shaped than round. The 70's Seven was bound to be controversial. For much of the sports-car-buying public, the new shape was inevitably too-much-too-soon or too-little-too-late. Seven *aficionados* simply went into shock. The trouble was, 1957 was long gone and the Seven was finding it hard to grow up.

The Series 4 body consisted of four fiberglass moldings: cockpit, bonnet and two front fenders. The main section was the cockpit, incorporating the rear fenders, tail panel, cowl and firewall. The seat recesses, luggage area and floor were molded in, as were the transmission tunnel and "door" sills. The cockpit section was slipped under the sheet metal scuttle; then bolted to the chassis by threaded bobbins imbedded in the fiberglass. The body color was impregnated in the fiberglass: yellow, red, white, blue, orange or lime green.

The bonnet, incorporating the frontal air intake and carb airscoop, was hinged at the front like the Jag XKE's. The obvious advantage was that the engine and cooling system could be exposed at the same time. Then too, with the classic Seven you never knew where to put the alloy bonnet cover: on the cockpit where it invited scratches or on the ground where someone could step on it. The Series 4 bonnet simply balanced in an open position. In theory, complete removal was quickly accomplished by removing two bolts through the hinges. In practice, the bolts were in an area exposed to water and quickly rusted in place.

The front fenders were bolted separately to the chassis. In early production, the turn indicators were fixed to the bonnet sides back of the air intake. On later versions they became part of the fender tops along with the running lights.

Turn indicators were fixed to bonnet sides on early Series 4's; later moved to fender tops.

Quadruple Linkage

Except for retaining the Escort axle of the Series 3, the rear suspension was a total departure from previous Sevens. Lotus gave the car a quadruple-link system. The ends of the axle were located by both a leading and a trailing arm. Lateral fixing was accomplished with an A-arm on the left side of the chassis. The ends of the arm extended to forward chassis pickups while the point was fixed to the axle. Some analysts described this system as using the axle as an anti-roll bar. Whatever the theory, there was sufficient roll resistance to lift the inside wheel in tight corners. The rear springs were coiled over the shock absorbers as in the previous series. Brakes were cast iron drums from the Escort/Cortina GT with a slightly larger diameter (nine inches) than the Series 3.

The front suspension was derived from the Lotus Europa. Both cars used the same springs, shocks and A-arms. For the first time, the Seven used double wishbones with separate anti-roll bar picking up the bottom of the shock absorber. The uprights were familiar Triumph pieces. Brakes were Girling trailing calipers with 8½-inch discs instead of 9. Wheels remained unchanged at 5½" × 13", but the steering gear became a Burman rack-and-pinion with 2¾ turns lock-to-lock.

Front suspension is derived from Europa. Still double wishbone but major change is separate anti-roll bar that picks up bottom of shock absorber.
Photo: Dennis Ortenburger

Exit Shiny Tranny Tunnels

The range of engines available with the Series 4 was the same as with the Series 3: the Escort 1300 GT, Cortina 1600 and Lotus twin-cam with optional Holbay modifications. The "Super Seven" nomenclature was dropped. With a 10.3 to 1 compression ratio and either twin Webers or Dellortos, the twin-cam gave 126 bhp at 6500 rpm and generated 113 pounds per foot of torque at 5500. (Later versions were claimed to produce 135 bhp, but these were usually supplied on order from Caterham.) The standard differential on all Series 4's was the 3.7 to 1. Also standard was the Corsair 2000E gearbox with ratios of 2.97, 2.01, 1.40 and 1 to 1. Lotus gave the Series 4 an engine-driven fan and moved the battery from the bonnet to the luggage area.

The interior of the Series 4 was kept simple and functional, while progressing toward the idea of a "proper" automobile. There was a nicely finished cockpit—all black carpeting, vinyl or rubber mat. Gone were the days of shiny alloy tranny tunnels and exposed chassis tubing. The increased interior dimensions plus individual seats with a greater

Arrgh! Once in the driver's seat, the Series 4 is more comfortable than previous models, but getting in and out is still a contortionist's delight—especially with the top up. Dr. Rasilewicz demonstrates finesse that comes with nine years of practice. Also note relocation of gas tank filler atop rear fender. *Photo: Dennis Ortenburger*

rake gave this Seven the most comfortable driving position yet. There was more leg room but space between the pedals was still too tight. Heel-and-toe maneuvers in the Series 4 were uncharacteristically difficult.

The steering wheel shrank from 14 to 13 inches in diameter with a PVC-covered rim. The new Triumph steering column was both collapsible and adjustable. Triumph also supplied column-mounted levers for high beam and flashers (on the left) and for turn indicators (on the right). The dashboard was redesigned to complement the 70's exterior. The speedometer, tachometer, oil pressure and water temperature

Nicely finished cockpit was kept functional, with controls easily to hand. Triumph steering column is both collapsible and adjustable.

gauge were arrayed on the dash in front of the driver. Fuel and ammeter gauges, rocker switches and ignition occupied a recessed center panel above the gear lever. There was even an optional ashtray and map light! The old inaccessible handbrake became the Elan "umbrella pull"—definitely an improvement, but now the brake caught taller drivers in the knee. Lap belts were standard, along with a diagonal harness mounted to the chassis.

Lotus redesigned the top and side windows to suit the new body. While not quite weatherproof, at least no water came in from below. *Two-speed* windshield wipers were standard, too! The side windows were equipped with sliding panels for ventilation. A heater with blower remained extra. The soft top lost the quarter window used on the Series

Innovation for Series 4 sidescreen was sliding panels to let in controlled amount of air. Folding top lost rear quarter windows. *Photo: Dennis Ortenburger*

3, but a rarely-seen fiberglass hardtop, with opening rear window, was optional. A roll bar, airhorns, tool roll, windscreen washers and Brand Lotus alloy wheels rounded out the optional extras.

Chapman Pulls The Plug

The new Seven was built by Lotus Components until their demise in 1970. Lotus Racing took over production until they, too, closed in 1971. From then until 1973 when Lotus ceased producing the Seven altogether, the Series 4 was added to the Lotus Cars production line. The end came when Chapman decreed austerity moves to curtail his huge financial losses. The Lotus Seven, even in fancy-dress, was holding the company back. Up-market Lotus Cars did not want to be reminded of their roots.

While it lasted, the Series 4 could be purchased factory-direct, through Graham Nearn's Caterham Cars, or from two additional dealers who had been appointed to help market the anticipated outpouring of Lotus Sevens. The works reported that the first car sold at the German Auto Show went to Ferruccio Lamborghini. Graham Arnold, Lotus Sales Director, immediately shot off a memo: "They must be having an economy drive at Lamborghini. If they have any Miuras perhaps they could send me one."

Initial kit prices were £895 ($2150) for the 1600 and £995 ($2400) for the twin-cam. By 1972 they had climbed to £1070 and £1295. The word "competition" fell from the ad writers' vocabulary, to be replaced by "sex appeal." Coincidental with the fun-car era was the age of the mini-skirt.

The American scene was thoroughly confused. The Series 4 was reported as having been Federalized, but in truth never was. Some dealers took advantage of a short-term government exemption and sold the car without difficulty. Even so, most of these were imported as kits in boxes marked "spare parts." The 1600 Cortina engine with emissions controls was usually purchased locally. Other dealers sold kits registered by the Department of Motor Vehicles as home-built, with no mention of Lotus whatever. A significant number of Series 4's came through Canada with doctored papers. The challenge was left to the owner in each state to discover which dodge was necessary to get his car "legally" on the road.

Right Car, Wrong Name

The Series 4 maintained the Seven's reputation for cornering like a bike. Still very stiffly sprung, the only problem on smooth surfaces was a tendency to lift the inside rear wheel in tight corners. A limited-slip Escort differential was a highly recommended option. Like all Sevens, the Series 4 understeered. On a flat, smooth and dry surface, the car was almost impossible to spin.

The car was slightly heavier than the Series 3. Curb weight was approximately 1200 pounds with the Escort engine; 1300 with the twin-cam. Performance was similar to the Series 3. The 1600 Cortina version topped out at just 100 miles per hour and got to 60 in under 9 seconds. Top speed of the twin-cam was up a few notches at 109 mph and acceleration down to about 8.5 seconds for 0 to 60. With Holbay options, the new Seven performed a little better than a similarly-engined Series 3, but with a penalty. The four-link rear suspension wasn't quite up to 135 bhp. All the fat rubber bushings would cause the axle to wind up and tramp excessively.

The Series 4 was continually compared with MG's and Spitfires and coming up short. The car wasn't nearly as refined. Road testers remarked at the considerable wind buffeting at any speed over 50. In

English autotest champ Stephen Stringer cruises in 1600-cc Seven.
Photo: Courtesy Anvil Turkeys Co. and "Drive In Silence" Co.

reality, though, the punishment was no worse than in earlier Sevens.
The separate body caused a few new rattles over rough surfaces. Brakes
and clutch, too, came under criticism for their action, but since pedal
travel was minimal, the complaints were minor. All in all, the Series 4
may have been right for the time. For Seven enthusiasts, though, the
car was called by the wrong name.

Still Too Fast To Race

Most production-class racing bodies felt the same way about the
Series 4 Seven as they had about the Series 3: the car was too fast to
race. As a result, activity in England was mostly limited to local sprints,
hill climbs and autotests. The car was competitive from the start. One
driver, Stephen Stringer, distinguished himself with his 1600-cc Series 4,
taking first overall in both RAC and BTRDA National Autotest Championships for 1978. Miss Felicity Kerr co-drove the car with equally
good results.

The American scene was limited to slalom and autocross, although
the SCCA classed the car for racing in D-Production. This was an interesting development, since, with few exceptions, the car could not
legally be imported. Tom Robertson prepared a Series 4 in 1979 and the
car showed good potential, though not making the National runoffs.

93

This is the Seven chassis as currently produced by Arch Motors for Caterham. Improvements include triangulation in lower plane of engine bay, reinforced transmission mount, and tabs for oil cooler installation forward of radiator.
Drawing: Paul Wasserboehr

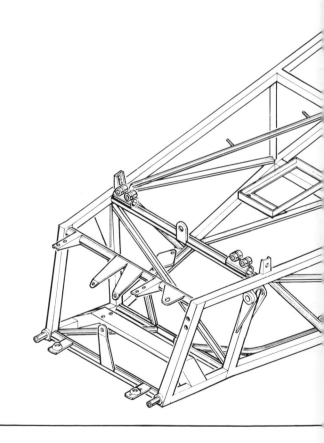

The Caterham Story

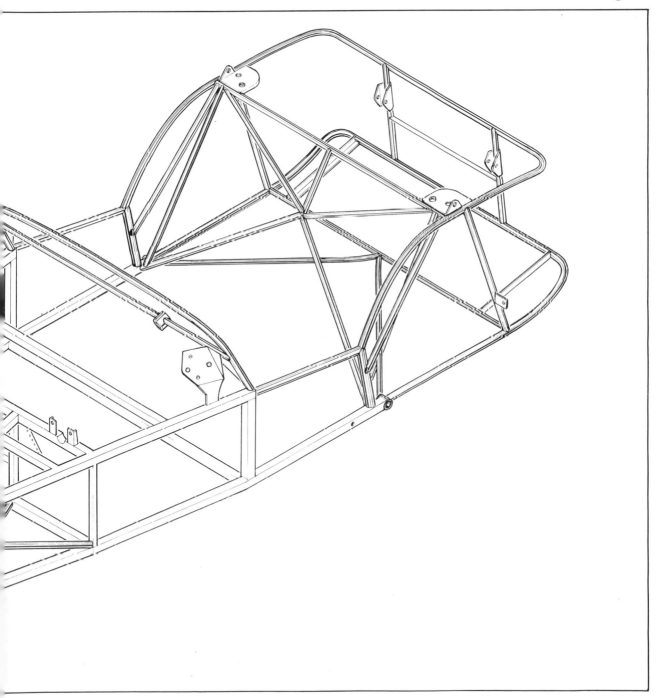

W hen full scale production of the Series 1 Seven began at Hornsey in 1958, Chapman was already making plans to reorganize Lotus Engineering Company Ltd. The move to the new factory at Cheshunt solidly identified Lotus as a bonafide automobile manufacturer. The next step was a proper marketing plan.

The following year Chapman toured the U.K. looking for dealers to handle the Elite and the Seven. One of the first "Lotus Centres" to sign on the dotted line was Caterham Car Sales in Caterham, Surrey, just south of London. Caterham was a modest operation run by enthusiasts who took Lotus cars very seriously. Service was their hallmark. They built a reputation as a reliable source for parts and information, and for genuinely caring about the cars.

Dealers Fall Out

Lotus Cars almost closed forever in 1959, in the manner of countless specialty car manufacturers before and since. Production economies, long range tooling, cost controls and the myriad other necessities for survival had been learned too slowly. When Chapman turned aggressive and announced the unbelievably low-priced Series 2 kit at £500, a steady flow of enthusiasts beat a path to his door, checkbooks in hand. Unfortunately for the Lotus Centres, the customers were buying factory-direct—there was no sense paying the dealer's mark-up. The price cut was a smart move for Cheshunt but a blow for the dealers. They fell out one by one.

Graham Nearn saved the Lotus Seven from extinction in 1966 and again in 1973. Bad luck for the caller—looks like Nearn's lips are sealed. *Photo: Mirco Decet*

Caterham had sold Lotus cars exclusively and couldn't survive with the new factory prices. The partners elected to call it quits and put the small shop up for sale. Graham Nearn, one of the principals, took over the company name and moved to a small house near the original shops. Nearn was an incurable car nut. He forged a successful business out of automobile repair and performance modifications and campaigned his Series 2 Seven on weekends. Nearn welcomed all his old Seven customers for servicing. As time progressed, the word rippled through Seven country that Nearn had a thorough understanding of the car's idiosyncracies and what to do about them.

One of Nearn's regular competitors on the race track was a Seven-owner named David Wakefield. Equally enthusiastic about the car, Wakefield joined forces with Nearn. The new Caterham Cars would specialize in repair, race preparation and sale of second-hand Lotus Sevens.

New Lease On Life

In the meantime, Lotus had stabilized again and new dealers were being signed on. The Elan was the thing; most firms didn't want to bother with the fiddley little Seven. The production rate had slowed to a trickle anyway—delivery time became so extended that many customers were lost to frustration. Nearn had occasionally picked up a new kit from the factory for special modification and was well aware of the situation. He was dismayed to see the source of both his income and his pleasure slowly wither on the vine. Recognizing the demand for the car, Nearn considered taking on the sale of new Sevens again.

The difficulty was locating either the Lotus Seven production line or the man in charge of it! When the company moved to Hethel in 1966, Lotus Components had virtually shoved the Seven parts in a corner with the rest of the scrap. Eventually, Nearn got in to see Chapman and advised him of the eager buyers climbing all over Caterham. Chapman agreed to resurrect Seven production and give sole distribution to Caterham Car Sales. There is little doubt that had Graham Nearn not made this expedition to Norwich, the Lotus Seven would have faded away by 1966.

The Series 2 Seven took a new lease on life and Caterham Cars became the focal point of Lotus Seven activity. For the next few years everything went smoothly, if slowly. Lotus Components cranked out a few cars and Caterham whisked them off to waiting enthusiasts. Not a cult car yet, but the Seven had all the makings: extraordinarily fun, utterly basic, limited production . . . and difficult to obtain.

Hand Over A Legend

In 1968 the Series 3 was introduced, incorporating a host of improvements. Nearn thought Lotus could have done more to strengthen the chassis, but at least Mike Warner, new head of Lotus Components, had guaranteed continued production. At the height of Series 3 production, Caterham was selling half a dozen kits a week. The Series 4 hit the dune buggy market in 1970 with an aggressive advertising campaign, and two additional dealers were signed to handle stepped up production. Then the wheel of fortune spun again, leaving Lotus Components closed and the Seven in the hands of Lotus Racing. The assembly line stumbled, finally grinding to a halt under Lotus Cars in early 1973. Chapman decided to lay the Seven to rest, but Graham Nearn had other ideas.

Caterham Car Sales agreed to purchase from Lotus all remaining Seven parts, jigs, molds, engines—the lot. In May 1973 a small

June 1973: Colin Chapman hands over Lotus Seven manufacturing rights to Graham Nearn of Caterham Car Sales. Future cars would still be "Sevens," but Lotus name had to be dropped. *Photo: Road & Track*

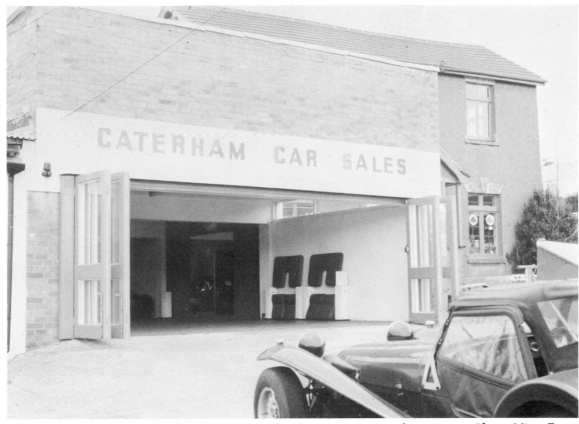
The unpretentious Caterham works in Caterham, Surrey. *Photo: Mirco Decet*

ceremony at the Pub Lotus in London made the deal official. Colin Chapman handed over a legend. The only hitch was that the car couldn't be called a Lotus any more. Nearn and Wakefield formed a new company named Seven Cars Ltd. to do whatever they wanted with all the bits and pieces.

Nearn's intention was to build cars and he even got Chapman to supply him the Lotus twin-cam engine. For a short period Caterham also sold Lotus Formula Fords, since part of the deal included the old Lotus Racing inventory. Caterham Car Sales ended up with 44 of the last Lotus racing cars ever sold to the general public.

Nearn and Wakefield began by assembling the Series 4. Nearn always thought the last Seven a pretty good car, and there seemed to be enough parts to set up an assembly line, at least for a while. They called their product the Caterham Seven. The car sold in completed form only: no kits. The 1300-cc version was available for £1195 ($2988); the Big Valve twin-cam for £1487 ($3700).

As time went on the suppliers became more and more leisurely about filling orders until a few items became impossible to obtain. Caterham's purchases were small and therefore relegated to a low priority. In mid-1974 Nearn and Wakefield got fed up with the production problems and called it *finis*. Approximately 60 Caterham Sevens had been built. About 50 of these were exported, most to Japan and Europe.

Return Of The Classic

While assembling the Series 4/Caterham Sevens, Nearn and Wakefield had not been deaf to pleas for a return of the classic Lotus Seven. A prototype Series 3 began to take shape in another part of the

At left and above are two views of the Caterham chassis with alloy panels riveted in place. Note additional forward tubes and reinforced tranny mount. On floor of assembly area can be seen the replacement for the Escort RS2000 axle, which is no longer in production. This is the heavy duty unit from the Morris Ital estate, and is some 33 pounds (15 kg) lighter than the RS2000, and has a ratio of 3.64 to 1. *Photos: Mirco Decet*

Caterham shops. The design was nearly identical to the Lotus Series 3, but incorporated a number of worthwhile improvements. The first priority was to improve the chassis. Tubes were added to strengthen the sides, engine bay and rear suspension pickups. The battery was lowered to prevent shorting on the alloy bonnet, and improved seat belt mounts designed. Caterham updated the rear axle by adopting the sturdy Escort RS2000 and added 6-inch Brand Lotus or Goodyear alloy wheels. Nine-inch disc brakes were used at the front on twin circuits with the rear drums.

The old Lucas taillights were traded for new rectangular Britax units incorporating stop, tail and turn indicators. Classic toggle-switches reappeared on the dash. The nose piece and bonnet were raised slightly for more engine clearance. A new close-ratio Ford 2000E gearbox was fitted, along with heavier steering rack mounting blocks. Caterham also added a Kenlowe-type electric fan for all cars and offered a redesigned roll-over bar, Smith's heater and air horns as options.

1977 model shows 3-in-1 Britax taillights and wider rear fenders that characterize the Series 3. Wheels are 6-inch Goodyear alloy. Gas tank filler has moved again. *Photo: Geoffrey Goddard*

Tiny gear lever is right where it should be for super-quick shifts. Caterham returned to classic toggles last seen on the Series 2 dash. *Photo: Geoffrey Goddard*

The specifications for the new/old Caterham Seven didn't make much difference to the cult, however. The important thing was that the real Lotus, check that, the real Super Seven was back. As to product identity, the Caterham nose badge was a derivation of the Lotus medallion with a "7" where "Lotus" used to be and Chapman's initials replaced with "CCS" for Caterham Cars Seven. Most buyers purchased Lotus motifs anyway.

The Super Seven from Caterham was the fastest production Seven of them all. Weight was variously quoted from 1162 to 1232 pounds. In any case, the Big Valve twin-cam took the car to almost 115 mph with 0 to 60 times in under 6 seconds.

In England, the only way around certain purchase tax and registration rules was to sell the car in kit form. That had never hindered sales before and certainly didn't now. Most export Sevens were completely assembled, however, and by 1979 roughly 75% of production was going to foreign customers. As the Caterham Seven approached the 1980's, the

The 1981 animal at the Surrey plant, with spare space frames piled up in back. Twenty-five years later, visible differences between this car and the first Lotus Seven don't even number ten. *Photo: Mirco Decet*

David Bettinson at speed, complete with CAN-AM spoiler. *Photo: Gerry Stream*

Lotus Ford twin-cam became harder to obtain and finally almost impossible. This wasn't surprising, since Lotus had last used the engine in the Europa, which was discontinued in 1975. Nearn and Wakefield saw the engine situation coming and negotiated with Ford to supply them the 1600-cc block. Another source supplies the twin-cam head and Caterham assembles the parts into an engine.

Today, demand for the car is stronger than ever. Production in 1979 was approximately 150 cars. At £5000 ($11,250), the price of a Caterham Seven in England reflects inflationary times but has had no effect whatever on orders. At the end of 1979 the waiting period for a Caterham Seven was almost six months. The goal for the 1980's is to contract with local suppliers for all components. With a consistent supply of parts, Caterham could easily increase car production to 200 units a year. The future looks bright indeed for the Seven. The only significant threats to Morgan-like survival take the form of safety regulations which are increasing in number and complexity worldwide. (True Seven enthusiasts would probably still prefer the car with railroad ties for bumpers.)

Seven Overseas

In the U.S., Sevens can be purchased in kit form from two Caterham agents: DSK Cars, Inc. in Marblehead, Massachusetts; and Dave Bean Engineering in Santa Barbara, California. The current model, in left-or right-hand drive, features a revised cooling system suitable for traffic use, higher-quality bodywork, and a slightly roomier interior. Buyers can obtain the chassis/body unit for about $3500 (1981 price) or a complete kit (less Ford engine and gearbox) for about $11,000. The close-ratio Ford 2000E gearbox is another $1200. Engines include the Vegan-tune big valve twin-cam ($2750) or Ford 1600 crossflow ($1400). Both dealers also sell a number of modification kits for improving early-model Lotus and Caterham Sevens.

Making the Seven street-legal is a matter between the owner and the motor vehicle department of his state. Most Sevens are properly registered as home-builts, which exempts them from federal safety requirements. However, modifications may be necessary to comply with the safety or emissions control regulations of a particular state.

Racing The Caterham Seven

In 1975 the Royal Automobile Club approved the Caterham Seven for racing in the Modsports Class. English Modsports featured production cars but allowed just about any modification, including altered bodywork, to cover the widest tires available. Most cars ended up about as wide as they were long. The Seven had to run the stock windshield and the clam shell fenders. Dave Bettinson accepted the challenge, dropped in a 154-horse Holbay twin-cam, put his top up and won the first championship round at Thruxton his first time out. The year progressed with protests and numerous unsportsmanlike maneuvers by fellow competitors. The RAC withdrew, and then restored, the car's eligibility. Despite the hassles, Bettinson captured a class championship in 1976 and a third overall in the Modsports standings.

While Bettinson's experience was hardly encouraging, Nearn tried petitioning the RAC to accept the Super Seven in standard production-class racing. The RAC replied, in essence, "No way, the car is too fast to race." Disappointed, but not blind to the advantages of adversity, Nearn printed tee shirts with the slogan: "The car that's too fast to race." The shirts are now collector's items worn only on special motoring occasions.

Redesigning to comply with new Dutch safety regulations made the Netherlands Seven of Joop Donkervoort roomier and zoomier. *Photo: Peter Ecury Collection*

Seven Knock-Offs

The persistent demand for the Lotus Seven in all parts of the world led to replicas fabricated in the most unlikely places. To build a Seven-like chassis, all that was really required was a welding rig, some mild steel tubing and a set of drawings or a Seven for reference. Numerous space frames with Seven heritage have been constructed and documented. Most were made to replace racing or road write-offs; a few evolved into specials. More interesting are the series-produced replicas built under license to Lotus or Caterham, or independent of both.

South American Seven

The first replica to be documented was a Series 3 constructed in Buenos Aires. Little is known about the Argentine Seven except that Lotus supplied the rolling chassis and the engine and drivetrain came from the Fiat 1500.

Spanish Seven

In 1975 Ben Heydrick, the Spanish importer of Porsche and BMW, decided to offer his customers something different in sports motoring. He would build a new car in the manner of the classic Hispano-Suiza. To this end, he formed a company with the imaginative name of Hispano-Aleman to manufacture the car. Heydrick called his creation the "Mallorca." The automobile turned out to be a Series 4 Seven under license to Caterham, which is about as far from the Hispano Suiza as a car could get.

The engine and drive train came from SEAT, Spain's major car-producer which uses many Fiat-licenced designs. Apparently, the body and chassis were altered slightly to accept the mechanicals. The price for the car was 300,000 pesetas (a lot of lira) or about $5,000. Only a few cars were built and none exported.

New Zealand Seven

A few months before Chapman decided to end Seven production forever, Lotus licensed Steel Brothers, Ltd. in New Zealand to build the Series 4. Lotus had always done well in New Zealand and Australia, but escalating import duties were a problem. A Series 4 buyer ordering his car from England could expect to pay over half again the car's U.K. price in tariffs.

Steel Brothers Ltd. is a heavy equipment manufacturer headquartered in Christchurch, New Zealand. The directors decided to enter the sports car business as a fun counterpoint to their larger-than-life earth-moving machines. Initially, the company bought complete kits from Lotus in lots of up to 50, to be assembled during slack periods in their regular production. Their workers enjoyed the diversion and, because their Series 4's sold at English prices (no tariffs added), sales were brisk. The venture into a completely different market was so successful that Steel Brothers elected to buy one of the two sets of jigs, molds and fixtures offered by Lotus when Series 4 production ended. (Caterham acquired the other set.)

Once all the bits and pieces were sorted, Steel Brothers took the opportunity to redesign the car for driving conditions down-under. Using Lotus jigs, they built the chassis from scratch, strengthening the front and rear suspension and engine bays with additional diagonals. The reinforcement, needed for New Zealand roads, added about 20 pounds to the weight of the frame.

The fiberglass body, subcontracted to a local fabricator, differed from the original by a slightly more bulbous rear fender line and a patterned air intake screen. Top, seats and trim were manufactured in-house, with

Steel Brothers used Lotus jigs to turn out New Zealand counterpart to Series 4, with strengthened chassis and detail changes such as patterned grille. This is the second-generation Super 907 twin-cam, which never reached production. *Photo: Steel Brothers Ltd. Collection*

subtle differences from the original. The top was given rear quarter windows to lessen the blind spots and the seats had additional padding and headrests. Side windows were more rigid and, with a vastly more authoritative closure, could almost be called doors. An opening compartment on the transmission tunnel and woodgrain contact paper on the dash completed the Steel Brothers refinements. Mechanically, the cars were identical with the Caterham Series 4 except that only the twin-cam engine was mounted.

Production was leisurely at about two cars a week—during the summer months, that is. In winter the line closed down and the workers reacquainted themselves with bulldozers and dump trucks. After two years and about 100 Series 4's, Steel Brothers began to feel the engine crunch as had Caterham. One day, the Ford twin-cam simply stopped coming. Unwilling to pack it in, they looked to alternatives.

The obvious preference was to stay with Lotus. Their powerful, economical and environmentally-clean Vauxhall-based "907" twin-cam was in full production for use in the Jensen-Healey, Lotus Elite, Eclat and Esprit. Lotus had their own engine manufacturing facility and could produce a steady supply. Steel Brothers set out to redesign the Series 4 body and chassis to accept the new engine.

A beautiful prototype was built that was entirely recognizable as a Series 4 Seven. The giveaway was a bulge in the right-hand bonnet side to clear the induction system. The chassis was modified to accept both the 2-liter 907 engine and the Lotus 5-speed transmission and the design worked extraordinarily well. Wider wheels were mounted and spring rates adjusted. Production would soon be a reality. Alas, legislation reared its well-meaning head. The government pronounced the car unsafe for the lack of anti-burst door locks, compliance plates, etc. etc. By the end of 1979, Steel Brothers reluctantly announced the Super 907 could not be built to comply with the new rules and the project would be abandoned. They haven't given up yet, however. The 1980's may still see an open two-seater sports car using a Lotus drive train, but the car won't be a Seven or even close to one.

Netherlands Seven

Joop Donkervoort is living proof that Lotus Seven enthusiasts are a breed apart. Until 1976 he operated the Dutch sales outlet for the Caterham Series 3 and was doing a steady business supplying most of Northern Europe with new Super Sevens. For most people the end would have come when the Ministry of Transport announced the car could no longer be imported. New Dutch laws followed the European trend toward minimum interior dimensions (Caterham's were too small) and required passive safety devices. In the case of the Seven, the gas tank had to be protected against rear-end collision.

Donkervoort looked at a bare chassis in his shop and studied the new laws. He decided to redesign the car to comply with the law. While he was at it, he would incorporate changes in response to his clients' most frequent criticisms. The new car would have a roomier cockpit and pedal area, even better handling, more luggage room, greater chassis rigidity and a more-easily serviced engine. Shrewd fellow this Joop Donkervoort, because most of his customer complaints would be resolved automatically by complying with the new regulations.

The first thing he did was truck a Series 3 chassis to the Dutch Technical University at Eindhoven. Donkervoort made clear that the character and the line of the car couldn't be changed; only improved. After a few stress calculations, a computer model (and some suspension theory supplied by Donkervoort), the results were a new Seven chassis

Joop Donkervoort (left) provides sense of scale for this Netherlands Seven outside Tienhoven plant. Seven-collector Peter Ecury is at right. *Photo: Peter Ecury Collection*

that would be both legal and comfortable for the foreseeable future. Back at his base at Tienhoven, Donkervoort set to work building the first European-legal Seven.

Few visual clues point to differences between Donkervoort's D-Type Super Seven and the Caterham version. Yet, the car is 2.73 inches longer in wheelbase and the chassis is 5.46 inches wider at the seat backs in the cockpit. The driver finds 3½ inches more leg room, 1¼ inches more head-room with the top up, and individual bucket seats. The engine and gearbox were moved 2¾ inches back in the chassis for better weight distribution. Springs were uprated and, similar to the Series 4, the Escort axle was located by four arms. In addition, a Panhard rod is also employed. Donkervoort claims absolutely neutral handling in corners using this set-up, with significantly better rear axle control than in the Caterham car.

The D-Type will actually carry luggage, because the single gas tank

Driver luxuriates in wide-bodied cockpit with bucket seats in Connolly leather. *Photo: Peter Ecury Collection*

110

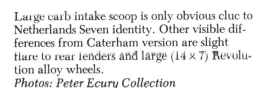

Large carb intake scoop is only obvious clue to Netherlands Seven identity. Other visible differences from Caterham version are slight flare to rear fenders and large (14 × 7) Revolution alloy wheels.
Photos: Peter Ecury Collection

has been replaced by twin aluminum units fitted ahead of the rear axle. Additional chassis rails under the cockpit and in the lower engine and transmission bays contribute to increased torsional rigidity. Body changes include a louvered bonnet and a large carb intake scoop. The rear fenders are flared ever so slightly to cover Revolution alloy wheels in 14-inch diameter by 7-inch width. The change from a 13- to a 14-inch wheel was to gain slightly better ground clearance. The wheels have the added effect of dominating the D-Type's appearance.

The Dutch Super Seven uses the Escort RS 2000 engine. (Donkervoort also builds a B-Type with Ford 1600 crossflow). The Escort motor is rated at 110 bhp at 5500 rpm. The performance puts the engine in the Lotus twin-cam league, but with a better parts and service situation.

In January 1981 Donkervoort introduced a new version specifically for export. The "Supereight," available only LHD, is powered by a Ford 2-liter OHC (Pinto/Cortina) bored out to 2.1 liters and fitted with a high-lift cam. The engine generates about 140 bhp and is reportedly faster than the Ford 1600 twin-cam.

9

Lotus engineer Hugh Haskell tries his sleeper on for size at Cheshunt in April 1962. Starting with a crashed Series 1, he redesigned the space frame, put on formula car suspension, flared the fenders and fitted wobbly-web mags. The result was nicknamed the "7½".
Photo: Duncan Steward Collection

Seven One-Offs

A ll Lotus Sevens are special—it's just that some are a bit more
outlandish than the rest. Whether for competition, pleasure motoring
or just to be seen in, a little modification here and there is part of the fun.

The Lotus 7½ Or 7/20

In early 1962 a very unusual Seven rolled out of the works at Cheshunt.
It was variously called the Lotus 7½ or the Lotus 7/20. The chassis
started life as a Series 1 and belonged to Wendy and Keith Hamblin, who
had purchased the car new in kit form. After a bad crash at Silverstone,
the Hamblin's idea was simply for the factory to restore it to original condition. However, Hugh Haskell, a project engineer at Lotus, had some
ideas for improvements up his sleeve. He convinced them to allow his
modifications and apparently persuaded Chapman to let him use various
bits and pieces out of the works surplus bins.

The first order of business was the chassis. Haskell redesigned the
space frame to resemble more the Lotus Eleven, with even better
triangulation except for the cockpit, which was essentially unchanged.

The front suspension was by double wishbone, but the anti-roll bar
picked up the *lower* member. Disc brakes were fitted, using Girling
leading edge, lightweight, AR calipers. The steering was Elite rack-and-
pinion placed back of the wheel center line with negative Ackerman
geometry. Wheels were 13-inch-diameter wobbly-web mags, the fronts
being Lotus 20 at 4½ inches wide and the rears prototype Lotus 22 at
5½ inches wide.

The rear suspension was fully independent and used a Lotus Eleven
alloy diff case with inboard disc brakes. Girling AR calipers were used

114

115

here as well, and like the Eleven were mounted in the leading edge position. Fixed length half-shafts and a lower wishbone provided lateral location for the Lotus 20 hub carriers. Extremely long parallel arms fixed longitudinal movement and extended to forward mounts on the outside of the alloy body work. Cycle fenders were used up front, but the rears were flat sections, bulged to allow suspension travel.

Independent rear suspension used fixed-length half-shafts with long parallel arms to fix longitudinal movement.
Photo: Dennis Ortenburger

The engine was a Cosworth 105E, and its 997 cc's gave 87 brake at 7200 rpm. A dry sump was used along with twin Webers and a Derrington 4-branch exhaust manifold. The engine was placed farther back than usual, apparently to negate some of the understeer, and angled so that the Webers fit inside the bonnet without the need for a scoop. Close ratio gears were fitted to the Sprite transmission. All in all it was one of the first and one of the best tricked-up Lotus Sevens.

As to the name for the Haskell creation, the boys in the shop called it a "Seven-and-a-half," a designation which the press quickly picked up. Others, however, saw that the car used the suspension from the Lotus 20 Formula Jr., hence that title. The lack of any special designation was encouraged by Lotus, because if the car was to be raced, the more confusion over its origin, the better.

Building a "sleeper" for production class racing was in fact Haskell's goal, and although a few eyebrows were raised at scrutineering, he usually pulled it off. The first regular drivers were Clive Lacey and Wendy Hamblin, but even Colin Chapman had a go in the car now and again. In 1962 the car captured best time of day at the Allard Owners Club speed trials. Lacey also scored at the BARC Goodwood sprints that year, and the 7½ could usually be expected to take BTD or a class win wherever and whenever it raced—apparently never finishing lower than fourth in its entire career. David Porter drove the 7½ regularly in 1963 and achieved wins on just about all of the English club circuits. In 1964 the car was acquired by Miss Natalie Goodwin and she took a second in the 1000-cc class at the BRSCC meeting at Snetterton.

Inevitably, a few of the enthusiasts who saw the 7½ wanted a copy. Haskell supervised the construction of four replicas, at least one being

Colin Chapman (at right) kneels beside 7½ at Silverstone pits. Chapman drove for six-hour relay, and the 7½ was fastest car on the track that day.
Photo: Duncan Stewart Collection

Bob Anderson drives Car #2, one of four 7½ replicas, at Zandvoort in 1963. Like the others, this inexact copy had Series 2 cowl and regulation rear fenders. Note LHD and Type 23 wheels. *Photo: Duncan Stewart Collection.*

left-hand drive. Although these were based on the Series 2, it is unknown to what extent they copied the original's chassis detail. Some obvious differences were, however, the Series 2 nose cowls (Hamblin's had the droop-snoot Series 1) and rear fenders.

As the rules got tighter in English production racing, the 7½ was forced to run in Formula Libra or open events, becoming less competitive though no doubt just as entertaining. In 1965 Duncan Stewart, an American Lotus Seven collector extraordinaire, found the Hamblin car and brought it to the U.S. It saw little use until the current owner, Dr. Stu Baumgard of Encino, California, purchased it in 1977 and embarked on a complete restoration. He was amazed to find the chassis in absolutely perfect order, requiring only stripping and paint. Dr. Baumgard has treated his 7½ to new alloy panels and lots of TLC in the detailing. His plans are for historic car racing in the 1980's.

In 1977, Dr. Stu Baumgard acquired the original Hamblin 7½ and embarked upon full restoration for street use and vintage racing. The chassis was stripped, painted and fitted with new alloy panels. Comparison with the original reveals that paint, polish, small bonnet bulge and roll bar are about all that distinguish the two. This has to be one of the most painstaking restorations around. *Photos: Dennis Ortenburger*

The Lotus Type "Three Seven"

This special Seven was designed in 1965 with similar intentions as the 7½, but with full works support—no pretext of kidding either press or scrutineer. The car was intended to do battle in the new Clubman Formula and given a Lotus type number because a short production run was planned. Officially, the car was named the Type 37, but it was usually referred to as the Lotus "Three Seven."

The Three Seven made its debut at the London Racing Car Show. Essentially it was a Series 2 but with significant differences. The chassis was strengthened by more triangulation, although not quite to the degree of the 7½. There was independent rear suspension with an Elite differential and inboard disc brakes using Girling leading edge alloy calipers. Fixed length half-shafts picked up the alloy hub carriers, but unlike the 7½, the lower links were two parallel arms. Fore and aft

Complex 5-link independent rear suspension system of Lotus Three Seven used fully-braced Elite differential, half-shafts, inboard disc brakes and five separate members to locate rear wheels. *Photo: Adrien Schagen Collection*

axle location was accomplished as on the 7½ with a pair of arms leading forward from the hub carrier. They were shorter in length than the earlier car and attached to the same vertical chassis tube as the normal single-link Series 2. With five separate members locating the rear wheels, questions of geometry were bound to arise, but rubber bushes apparently allowed the right amount of compliance and the system worked extremely well.

Front suspension was by double wishbones and a separate anti-roll bar. The steering rack was located behind the wheel center line as on the 7½, and the wheels were also 13-inch Lotus wobbly-web mags. The

Lotus Three Seven debuts at London Racing Car Show. Body is a hybrid, with alloy cycle fenders in front and fiberglass wings at rear. Wheels are 13-inch wobbly webs. *Photo: Adrien Schagen Collection*

rear fenders were widened Series 2 fiberglass items and the fronts were alloy cycle-type. The engine was a dry sump 116E Cosworth Ford with power output rated at 125 bhp.

The prototype was raced by John Berry, a Lotus employee, and he dominated the Clubman Class for several years. Unlike the production classes this one was wide open, and Berry's success ought to have guaranteed a good market for replicas. Lotus, however, had second thoughts, apparently due to production demands brought by the Lotus Elan. In addition, the Three Seven was going to cost about $4000, and at that figure was over twice the price of a 1500 Super Seven in kit form. The Three Seven thus wound up being a one-off, but interestingly, several Series 2's exist today with the 37 five-link independent rear suspension.

The Lotus Seven S

In 1969 Lotus Components put together an attention-getting Series 3 for the Racing Car Show. Called the Seven S, it was an exercise in seeing just how fast and luxurious they could make the car. "Luxurious" seems a definite *non sequitur* applied to the Seven, but what else would one call a white leather interior? The seats were heavily padded buckets and the white color was used for the top and interior panels. Both cockpit and trunk had black carpeting, trimmed in white, and the steering wheel was leather rimmed. A heater and—sacrilege—push-button radio were also fitted. Paint was Rolls-Royce metallic maroon and the face of the alloy dash panel was polished. Chromed suspension, air horns, tinted windscreen, a wooden gearshift knob and 5½-inch-wide Dunlop alloy wheels wearing Dunlop SP Aquajet tires completed the visuals.

A 1600 crossflow was fitted but Holbay gave it their CFR (FR for fast road) treatment. The head was modified with porting and flow work and had a 10 to 1 compression ratio. Twin Weber 40-DCOE's, a 4-branch exhaust manifold and a high lift R120 cam shaft complimented the head work. The bottom end was balanced and used special Hepolite pistons. The engine produced 120 bhp at 6200, pushing the Seven S from 0 to 60 in 7.2 seconds. Top speed was approximately 108 and fuel consumption was in the range of 18 to 23. The Seven S was fast, but not much quicker than the old 109E Super Seven or for that matter the standard 1600 crossflow. Obviously, the extra fittings added the few pounds which made all the difference.

Incredible as it seems there was real interest in both the performance and the pizazz of the Seven S, which the press dubbed the "Ultimate Seven." Lotus Components put a rather stiff price tag of £1600 on the car in assembled form only, figuring that would scare off any customers, but when Graham Nearn showed them cash deposits they were obliged to fill the orders. Reportedly a dozen were made, all with special chassis numbers, but exactly how many rolled out of Norwich is unknown.

The Lotus Seven X

Another driver to do well driving the Three Seven was Tim Goss, who shared a championship title in the Clubman class in 1969. As the new season approached he commissioned Lotus to build an updated version. The works apparently agreed to the project in order to test engineering innovations that would be used in the Series 4.

The Seven X chassis thus resembled more a Series 4 than a Series 3, specifically in the use of alloy-clad box sections. Otherwise the car looked very similar to the advanced Clubman racers seen in both England and Australia. The basic shape was wide and squat, accentuated by a rectangular air intake. Front and rear fenders were cycle type, but the rears scribed an arc of only about 90 degrees. Wheels were supplied by Team Lotus and were eight inches wide in front and ten inches wide at the rear.

The front suspension was by double wishbones with a separate anti-roll bar. An independent arrangement was used at the rear with an Elan diff and double U-jointed half-shafts. Rear uprights were Lotus 61 (Formula Ford) and were located by top links (one each side) and lower wishbones. Outer trailing links, similar to the standard Series 2 and 3 cars, fixed the uprights longitudinally. Disc brakes were fitted outboard at each wheel.

The engine was a Holbay-tuned 1600-cc Ford crossflow that put out a reported 140 bhp and was mated to an Elan close-ratio gearbox. The combination of light weight, wide track, willing engine and talented driver netted another championship for Tim Goss and Lotus in the Clubman in 1970.

The Seven Coupes

Every Seven owner has experienced frozen elbow and numb ears in fierce weather and must have wished for something more substantial overhead than sailcloth. In 1963 an enterprising British fiberglass shop, Fibrepair by name, decided to do something about the annoyance and make a few quid as well. They designed and built a fiberglass hardtop with gullwing doors for the Series 2 Seven. It sold for a very reasonable

And now for something completely different . . . Fibrepair's gullwinged hardtop attached to Series 2 for more complete weatherproofing. It sold for a reasonable £77.
Photo: Adrien Schagen Collection

122

Honeymoon Seven departs on 300-mile trip with fortnight's
luggage in place. *Photo: Rod Leach Collection*

Honeymoon Seven

Rodney Leach operates "Nostalgia: Specialist in Historic Sports Cars" in England and sells all manner of grown-up toys, from alloy-bodied Jag XK120's to 427 Cobras. He's gained a fine reputation dealing in top quality gear and "discovering" some very interesting automobiles. He also came close to meeting his maker in a Seven coupe.

In 1969 Leach purchased a Super Seven with a unique alloy hardtop and sidescreens. The windows in the latter were ¼ inch plexiglass, and only the driver's side had a small circular shutter for ventilation. A system of sliding bolts held the whole thing together, taking several minutes to undo. Once inside and buttoned up it was rather like the Apollo space capsule as designed by H. G. Wells.

After getting the car, Leach drove over to his fiance's to show off. Though suffering from a slipped disc in her back, she performed the necessary contortions to get in and go for a ride. Everything went fine until they got trapped in Friday rush hour traffic. Trapped is not just a figure of speech in this case, for, as Leach recounts, "Suddenly large blue sparks flashed from under the dash and great clouds of thick, acrid smoke from an electrical fire swirled around the cockpit." A hasty exit was impossible and Leach says he doesn't know what might have happened if "some enterprising passer-by hadn't spotted the problem, run into a tool shop alongside . . . borrowed a giant pair of metal shears and . . . snipped us out of the top!"

The fire was extinguished and temporary repairs made, but on the ride home the entire top section blew off at 60 miles an hour, disappearing "backwards into the air and thence over some tall hedges into the darkness beyond . . . "

Now, if there is a common thread to Seven owners, it must be devotion bordering on the unbelievable. Despite this disastrous start, Leach didn't let the car go as a bad choice. Instead he ordered "a proper hood and sidescreens" and elected to use the Seven as his honeymoon transportation. Strapped in the spare tire's place went a large suitcase for the three week trip—and they were off! But though the honeymoon was just beginning for Rod and his wife, it was over for the Seven. The first stop was a five star hotel in Bath. At 11:30 p.m. Rodney was summarily called to the front desk. The hotel's request was simple and direct: "Remove from our premises the means of transport you have chosen to employ. It has offended some of our other guests."

Not that a honeymoon in a Seven didn't have some advantages. On the last day, the unfortunate Mrs. Leach again slipped a disc and had to be swathed in plaster from armpit to hip. An ambulance was readied for the long journey home, but then the hospital staff spotted the Lotus Seven. Says Leach: "So rigidly was my wife held in between the transmission tunnel and body sides, (the doctors) deemed the Seven a perfect means of transport for her condition. We drove the 300 miles home without a break."

Neither smoke, nor fire, nor insult deterred the Leaches' affection for their car. They drove the Seven regularly for the rest of the year. It was snow that finally broke them down—the sight of the car buried under the snow outside their flat. The scene brought back vivid memories of "inserting Mrs. Leach through the gap between hood and body on some dark, wet and cold return from the cinema," and they decided to do without "the more notorious part of the Seven's endearing character." Ah well, nothing lasts forever.

123

£77 and even saw use on the race tracks. This happened at the hands of some of their bolder customers who passed their Sevens off as small GT's—with great success.

The other coupe pictured was a Series 1 built in England in 1959 and constructed as a 1000-cc Grand Touring car. Little is known about the builder or history except that the car was campaigned occasionally until about 1961. The top predates Fibrepair's and was made of fiberglass bonded directly to the chassis. The car found its way to Holland in 1975

Peter Akkerman's one-of-a-kind Seven coupe dates from 1959. The enveloping fiberglass top was bonded directly to the Series 1 chassis, replacing original rear panel and fenders. Cosmic alloy wheels are recent addition. *Photos: Peter Akkerman*

and passed through the hands of Peter Ecury, Northern Europe's most avid Lotus collector. The current owner is Peter Akkerman of the Netherlands. A full restoration is underway, and this car is certainly one of the most radical looking Sevens ever built.

The Seven Pickup

Bob Kroonenberg purchased a D-Type Seven in Holland in 1977 and was so delighted with the car it became his daily transport. He learned to put up with just about every Seven inconvenience and peculiarity but one—he was freezing his cookies off in those brisk Dutch winters.

He decided to build a coupe top, but one which allowed easy access to the luggage area. Kroonenberg considered hatchbacks with an access panel behind the seats, but didn't like either the inconvenience or the weather-sealing problems. Instead he opted for one of the most unusual special Sevens, the pickup. The removable top is made of vinyl-covered alloy. Doors are lockable gullwings. The pickup "bed" is the normal Seven luggage area, but with a hinged cover which is lockable. A rack was added to the top side to carry weatherproof parcels. Other interesting features are running boards which join the front and rear fenders and bucket seats covered with Connolly leather.

The DSK Turbo Seven

David Kaplan and Clayton Seitz of DSK Cars, Inc. (see Chapter 12) played with the idea of building a state-of-the-art Seven chassis for

A Lotus Seven with running boards? Seven pickup is modified
Netherlands D-Type with removable vinyl-covered alloy top,
gullwings and hinged boot cover with carrying rack. *Photos:*
Peter Ecury

some time as a means of promoting their Seven product line and expertise. The chassis and suspension systems took several years of on-again-off-again development, and included the assistance of the Massachusetts Institute of Technology and noted race prep genius Carroll Smith.

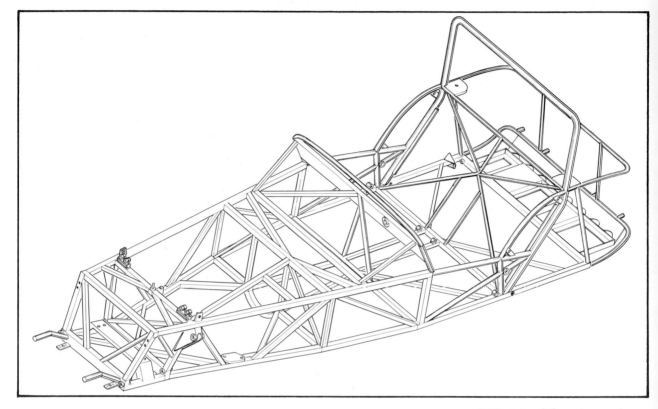

The space frame is a Caterham Series 3, but with about 100 pounds of additional bracing. Up front, diagonals were welded in to triangulate the suspension bay. Longitudinal floor rails run underneath the prop shaft tunnel, which incorporates a tubular gearbox mount. The cockpit received particular attention, with the addition of diagonals under the seats, a roll-over bar that encircles the inside chassis and a dash hoop that is triangulated and structural. The chassis sides have new braces and the rear suspension diagonals were reversed to accommodate a revised suspension system.

The front suspension features double wishbones with the lower member triangulated. The top wishbone is adjustable by threaded spherical rod ends, and the anti-roll bar is a separate component with an adjustable link to the lower wishbone. As a result, the system is adjustable for camber, castor and roll stiffness.

The rear suspension uses a live axle from the Escort but features a Panhard rod and twin trailing arms picked up at each side of the chassis. An anti-roll bar is mounted to the lower arms and can be changed without removing the wheels or raising the car. Both the rear trailing arms and the Spax shock absorbers front and rear are fitted with threaded spherical rod ends for adjustability and compliance.

The brakes are 9-inch discs at the front and 10-inch by 2-inch drums at the rear, with separate circuits and an adjustable bias. Brake lines are braided stainless steel. Spring rates were increased by 50% on all corners and the 6-inch wide KN Jupiter alloy wheels wear Pirelli 205/60 VR rated 13-inch P6's.

DSK state-of-the-art space frame is fully braced and triangulated with integrated roll bar and dashboard hoop modified into structural member. Additional bracing adds 100 pounds to chassis weight.
Drawing: Paul Wasserboehr

Other details include a foam-filled fuel cell, braided stainless steel fuel and oil lines, aircraft Teflon wiring and circuit breakers, competition seat belts and aircraft grade fasteners throughout.

The body has all the familiar alloy panels, but the fender shape and front end profile were developed by MIT's Aeronautics and Astrophysics Department. Bumpers are integrated into the profile, as are a front spoiler and fender pontoons—all in the interest of streamlining. An air foil section on top of the windscreen is credited to a certain Professor Larabee at MIT. This helps limit cockpit turbulence (recall Frank Costin's similar ideas with the Series 1).

The engine is as special as the chassis, and turbocharging provides just the right ingredient. An uprated Ford Kent 1600-cc crossflow carries a boost pressure of 10 psi maximum. The Turbo utilizes a single Weber 40-DCOE, and the engine has forged Arias pistons (8.4 to 1 compression) and dry sump lubrication. Power is rated at 180 at 6000. A side benefit of the dry sump is the elimination of the oil sump and an instant gain in ground clearance. The engine uses a close-ratio Escort gearbox and was moved three inches back for better weight distribution and to allow the use of an engine-driven fan.

All in all this chapter on special Sevens could hardly be concluded by a more worthy example. The Seven S may have been called the Ultimate Seven, but the DSK Turbo should rightfully claim that title. Lest any Seven owners feel left out, DSK offers most of the Turbo sub-systems as modifications or updates for Series 2, Series 3 and Caterham cars. (See Chapter 12 and Appendix 1).

The ultimate in Seven-power:
DSK turbocharged 1600-cc
crossflow with single Weber,
forged Arias pistons and dry sump
puts out 180 bhp at 6000 rpm.
Photo: Courtesy DSK Cars, Inc.

10

The aerodynamic Marcos coupe of Frank
Costin and Jem Marsh was incredibly
ugly but went like stink.
Photo: Frank Costin Archives

Seven Spin-Offs

Almost from the beginning, the Lotus Seven achieved a status envied by other builders—not in the way Ford envies Chevrolet, but the way a second place driver looks at the car that came in first. The Lotus Seven had been extraordinarily successful in defining and then satisfying the enthusiast's desire. Quite naturally, others wanted a piece of the action, too. There were many attempts to beat the Seven at its own game, in terms of road performance, price or racing success. All the imitators shared a strong family resemblance, which was probably the highest compliment they could pay—each sought to be different and yet the same. While all had some success, none have enjoyed the sustained popularity of the Seven. The English Value Added Tax (VAT) crippled most of the very small specialty and fun car builders in the mid to late 1970's. Only the Lotus Seven and the highly adaptable Dutton had the momentum and following to survive. It's tough to take on a legend!

The Marcos

The ancestor of the swoopy Marcos GT cars of the late sixties was designed and built for one purpose: to humble the Lotus Seven. Aerodynamicist Frank Costin had used the prototype Seven on the road for a time and was delighted with the concept. He was appalled at the lack of weather protection and the wind turbulence in the cockpit. The idea of an inexpensive, lightweight, high performance sports car was appealing, but to suit Costin the car had to be a coupe.

A few specifications were jotted down, but nothing more was accomplished until 1959, when Costin encountered Jem Marsh. Marsh ran Speedex Castings and Accessories Ltd., catering to the aftermarket performance accessory trade, and was active in 750-cc racing. When, inevitably, the conversation came round to motorsport, Costin told Marsh of his ideas for a GT coupe patterned after the Lotus Seven. Racing the car would provide publicity and encourage sales. Marsh wanted to expand Speedex and the manufacture and sale of such a car coincided perfectly with his plans. An agreement was struck and Costin set to work on the design.

Unique wooden monocoque was a natural for Costin: strong, economical and guaranteed leak-proof. *Photo: Frank Costin Archives*

What he ended up with was rather startling: a wooden monocoque. Considering Costin's experience with aircraft design, the idea was perfectly natural. A timber structure could be built much less expensively than a tube chassis. Tooling was simpler, special skills weren't required in manufacture and a properly-designed monocoque would have immense strength. With a fully enclosed body/chassis, only the doors would need weatherproofing.

All-up weight of 900 pounds plus Costin aerodynamics meant the Ford-powered Marcos could out-run the Seven. Independent front suspension, live rear axle and front cycle fenders followed the Lotus lead. Only two of these cars were built.
Photo: Frank Costin Archives

The prototype had independent front suspension, a Ford 997-cc engine, an Austin live rear axle, front cycle fenders and negative Ackerman steering. Other than chassis construction and the coupe configuration, the design followed the Seven concept very closely. Even so, certain Costin-inspired aerodynamic elements were incorporated, such as a fully-ducted radiator and cockpit ventilation. The car ended up incredibly ugly but went like stink—faster than the Lotus Seven. An all up weight of close to 900 pounds (body/chassis weighed but 145) and better aerodynamics made all the difference. While the prototype Marcos (the name a contraction of Marsh and Costin) was being detailed for its official debut, a second car was built for race driver Bill Moss. Moss scored nine consecutive wins with his Cosworth-tuned 1-liter Ford "Super Marcos" and captured five lap records in the process.

For a few months it looked like the Seven's racing days were numbered, but Marcos chose to capitalize on the sensational racing success by changing their marketing plan. Sensitive to the "ugly duckling" label pinned on by the press, Marsh and Costin decided to reshape the body and market a "poor man's Lotus Elite." The third car had all-enveloping bodywork and any relationship with the Lotus Seven was lost. Costin was involved with a total of eleven Marcos cars before leaving the company for other projects. He'd made his point though: a Seven imitator could be made weatherproof, and faster in the bargain. The technology was admittedly radical, though, especially for 1959.

The Elfin Clubman

Early Clubman racing was tailor-made for the Lotus Seven and the car actually defined the class in Australia. Numerous one-off specials were built in England and elsewhere but none so closely resembled the Seven as the series-produced Elfin Clubman.

Built in Australia by Garrie Cooper, the car was designed from the start to be a near carbon copy of the Series 2 Seven. Cooper began manufacturing his Elfin Racing cars in the 1950's, but the first serious attempt at series production came in 1959 with the Elfin Sport. This car happened to be a mirror image of the Lotus Eleven and was extremely successful in both competition and the marketplace. With no import duties attached, the car was a cut-rate Lotus (almost).

In late 1961, Cooper introduced the Elfin Clubman with the same philosophy—here was a replica of a proven winner at substantially less cost than the U.K. original. Cooper earned a reputation for selling quality products with his Sports and the Clubman reaped the same kind of praise. Overall, the car was just a little bit better than the Seven.

Elfin Clubman is hard to distinguish from the Seven, but conical bonnet and nose cowl are telltale signs. Bonnet is hinged at the scuttle for easier maintenance. Note brake cooling ducts on rear fenders. This is Michael Claridge driving at Winton in June 1979. *Photo: John Blanden*

From the rear the series-built Elfin is virtually impossible to tell from a Seven. Only clues are passenger side cubby-hole for storage and thicker clam-shells.
Photo: Tony Caldersmith Collection

The obvious difference in appearance was a conical bonnet and nose cowl, but Cooper scored marks for hinging the bonnet at the scuttle for easier maintenance. Front fenders were clam shells, albeit with a slightly different curvature than the Seven's. Constructed of thicker fiberglass, they, too, were an improvement on the original.

The windscreen and cockpit were pure Seven, but a passenger-side cubby hole for maps and gloves was a nice touch. The rear bodywork was Lotus again, except brake cooling ducts were placed in the leading edge of the rear fenders. The Clubman became noted for its fit and finish. Cooper used only the best materials and close manufacturing tolerances meant assembly was hassle-free and professional in appearance.

The chassis, including alloy panels, was patterned after the Series 2 Seven. The rear suspension, however, followed Series 1 practice in that the live axle (Austin A 30 or Farina A 40 in origin) was located by twin trailing arms and a Panhard rod. A departure from Seven design appeared at the front where the Elfin employed unequal-length wishbones, adjustable for camber and castor, but without an anti-roll bar. Steering was by rack and pinion with an adjustable column. Drum brakes were standard with front discs optional.

The choice of engines included the Cosworth 109E, BMC "A" series, Coventry Climax "FW" series, Ford 10, Consul and Fiat. The basic kit including body and chassis sold for £300 ($840). The top of the line (Cosworth 109E) went for £1375 ($3850), completely assembled but for the installation of engine and tranny—another Elfin touch that made "do-it-yourself" construction a piece of cake.

Although very successful in racing, the Elfin Clubman enjoyed a

134

relatively short career. Cooper had introduced a Formula Jr. along with the Clubman and, shortly thereafter, a sports racer similar to the Lotus 23. These cars stretched his manufacturing capabilities and the Clubman had to be sacrificed. Cooper's products continue to impress buyers with detailing and competitiveness. If you're in the market for a 1980's Formula Atlantic or F5000, you need only look to Australia to find the Elfin reputation still holds.

The Lotus Seven wasn't seriously threatened again until the American-inspired dune buggy craze hit England in the late 1960's. There the movement took two directions. One arm paralleled the VW-based, fiberglass-tubbed beach buggies and the other approached the street racer—clearly Seven territory. The "fun car" period created an entire industry devoted to completely impractical automobiles that were meant to be shown off before a suitably appreciative (female) audience. Lotus responded with the Series 4. All in all, "fun cars" was a lighthearted movement that would stumble with the advent of the VAT in 1973 and collapse with the first Arab oil crisis in 1974.

Early Dutton D-Type. *Photo: Alternative Cars*

The Dutton

Of the dozens of open two-seaters that appeared, the first to capitalize on the Lotus Seven's identity was the product of Tim Dutton Woolley in Sussex, England. Woolley built his first car in 1969 out of a strange assortment of parts, including a few from a Lotus Eleven and a few from a Sunbeam Alpine. As will be seen, imagination in parts sources would become a Dutton trademark. Woolley was spurred to series manufacturing when he assembled a friend's Lotus Seven kit. The exercise convinced him that he could build a similar vehicle for much less money.

In 1970 Woolley designed his Seven-imitator, the Dutton P1. Following Norwich practice, the Dutton was given a tube frame with alloy panels and bonnet. The nose cowling, front fenders and tail section were made of fiberglass. The rear body section featured an upswept spoiler and a hinged trunk lid. Viewed from the front, the car strongly resembled the Series 4 Seven. The P1 was designed to use the engine, drive train and suspension from early Sprites or MG Midgets.

The Dutton kit differed markedly from the Lotus original. The chassis, body panels, dash and windscreen were the only bits supplied. The price was very attractive at £200 ($480), but the customer had to be a skilled mechanic to procure and assemble the electrics, power train and suspension to complete the car. Fewer than a dozen P1's were made, due to the increasing value of bug-eyed Sprites, but Woolley was sufficiently encouraged to design its successors: the Dutton B-Type and B-Plus.

The B-Series differed from the P1 as follows: the chassis was strengthened, a power bulge appeared on the bonnet (a one-piece forward-hinging fiberglass affair incorporating the nose cowling), the front fenders were altered to include running lights, and headlights turned rectangular. Other than the headlights and upswept tail, the Dutton was once again pure Lotus Seven.

The big news about the B-Series was adaptability: the car used an astonishing variety of engines and suspension systems. The car could be assembled with Ford or Alfa twin-cams, BMC A-Series, Triumph 1200, 2-liter Ford Pinto, 3-liter Capri V-6, or Ford 1600 crossflow! Suspensions from Triumph sedans and Spitfire, as well as several from Ford, could be fitted. As a result, the Dutton always looked a little "bitsa" and it is doubtful two cars were ever exactly alike. By 1974 the Dutton had increased in price to £300 ($750)—still a bargain, as long as you knew your way around a tool box. In 1975, Dutton offered a "Malaga" body option, which incorporated circular headlights into the fender moldings to give the car more of a Morgan-like appearance. The current model, the Phaeton, was introduced in 1978. Available in either right- or left-hand drive, the car still accepts a wide variety of engines (including BMC, Triumph, Ford, Alfa, and Fiat), transmissions and rear axle assemblies. Front suspension is from the Triumph Spitfire. Rear suspension is quadruple link coil-over-shock.

The price of a Phaeton varies according to degree of completion. A basic component package consisting of space frame, roll bar, aluminum side panels, unpainted fiberglass body sections and unmounted windshield is available in the United States for $2995 (1981). The above plus installed rear 4-link suspension, steering column, pedal assembly and taillights runs to $3650. The most complete package, with everything furnished and installed except engine, transmission, driveshaft, radiator, tires and wheels, comes to $6699. Compared with the $11,000 required for a Caterham Seven kit (less engine and gearbox), the price no doubt explains the fact that the company sold over 500 automobiles worldwide

Highly adaptable Dutton started life as Series 4 look-alike with spoiler, but evolved along its own inimitable lines. Only Seven spin-off to survive the 70's, the Dutton has gone on to become the largest D-I-Y sports car manufacturer in the world.
Photo: Courtesy Dutton Cars., Inc.

in 1980. As their advertising is quick to point out, this accomplishment makes Dutton Cars, Ltd. the "world's leading manufacturer of unassembled sports cars." In the United States and Canada, Dutton kits are available from Dutton Cars, Inc. in Knoxville, Tennessee (see Appendix).

The Jeffrey

While the Dutton appealed to the budget-minded, imaginative and skilled kit-builder, the Jeffrey rated with performance-oriented enthusiasts. The story of the Jeffrey's development has a familiar ring. George Jeffrey was an engineer, active in the 750 Motor Club. He'd built numerous specials for 750, Formula 1200 and Formula Vee class racing. He designed the Jeffrey J4 in answer to requests for road-going versions of his racing cars.

The lightweight, rigid chassis was adapted from the Formula 1200 car. As with the Dutton and Lotus Seven, alloy panels clothed the chassis sides and undertray. Steering was by rack and pinion; the suspension was independent in front via unequal length A-arms and coil over shocks. At the back, a Ford axle was located by Panhard rod and four leading links. The all-fiberglass body was patterned after the Series 4 Seven. Sold only as a kit, the Jeffrey J4 was set up for Ford pushrod engines up to 1600 cc's. About 30 were built with prices ranging from £150 ($360) for body and chassis to £400 ($960) for body and chassis plus suspension, electrics, weather equipment and gas tank. Although test reports called the ride extremely stiff, insiders were quick to appreciate the superbly rigid chassis and well sorted suspension.

Encouraged by the demand, Jeffrey announced the J5 in 1973. The visible differences were a restyled body shape that was more curvaceous and an air intake remarkably similar to the Lotus Mark 6's. In overall line, the J5 was less like the Seven. Great care was taken in the molding and the finish was reported as exceptionally good. The chassis was basically the same but for changes in attachment points and brackets for easier assembly. The engine selection did not differ from the earlier car.

Inevitably, the J5 wore a higher price tag than the J4. Considering that the kit included everything except engine, drive train and wheels, £500 ($1200) was still a good price. Unfortunately, the VAT, paperwork and normal production headaches took away all the fun. In late 1973 George Jeffrey packed up shop, and the Jeffrey faded from the scene.

Early Jeffrey J4. *Photo: Alternative Cars*

Jeffrey J5, last of the breed. *Photo: Alternative Cars*

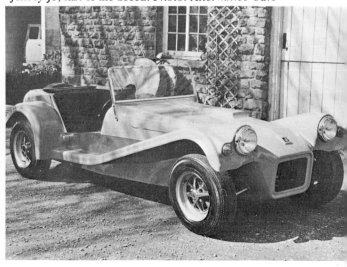

11

The Mazda-powered Seven of Jim and Judy
Gallagher — perhaps the fastest
ever built (zero to 60 in 4.5 seconds!).
Photo: Dennis Ortenburger

Racing Today: Still On The Top

Few automobiles fit the elusive definition of "sports car." For one thing, the concept changes a little with each generation. But in the early 1960's the Lotus Seven came closer to defining the term than any other car. From the beginning, the emphasis was on sport-racing and the Seven's use on the road was almost tongue-in-cheek. Road testers applied the terms "spartan" and "stark," but the joke was on them. All that was ever done was make a race car street legal and give a hint of road-going identity. The reason Seven owners smile a lot is they know what they're driving on the public roads is really a Formula Junior/Clubman/Formula Ford/Modsport race car with license plates.

What made the Sevens good in 1957 still holds true today: power to weight. The fact that they handle and stop is frosting on the cake. No wonder the car survived the fun car craze to line up again on the starting grids! Competitive sporting opportunities for the Seven include SCCA road racing, slaloming or autocrossing, and historic/vintage car racing. This chapter is a look at the state of the art in Seven competition today.

SCCA Road Racing With Tom Robertson

When Tom Robertson captured the United States D-Production Championship for 1977 in his Lotus Super Seven, he had been competing for 12 years. His string of racing cars included an MG, Lotus Eleven, Stanguellini Formula Junior and a host of Sprites. Robertson had first picked a Lotus Seven for 1975 because he liked the Marque and thought Sevens could be winners. By 1979 he had prepared and raced three of them.

Why On Earth Pick A Seven?

After 1977 everyone agreed the Lotus Seven was just the car to beat the new TR7—but that was after Robertson had done it. (See page 65 .) Before then everyone thought he was crazy to choose a 20-year-old design to do battle with British Leyland. Robertson was a thinking man's driver. Upon analyzing the class, he figured the Seven could be pared down to a thousand pounds, half that of the competition. The Seven handled well to begin with, so any development would net even better cornering power. Acceleration would be good, too. The only thing the Seven would give away would be top speed. Not much could be done about aerodynamics, but the SCCA allowed removing the headlights and adding a front spoiler. The spoiler tended to neutralize the lift generated by the fenders which, according to rules, had to be the clam shells. Actually, the Lotus Seven was more a race car to begin with than anything else on the grid, but structural modifications were in order.

Jim Gallagher at the wheel of his Rotary Seven. He has reason to smile. *Photo: Dennis Ortenburger*

Like most Seven owners/racers before him, Robertson had learned the hard way about chassis breakage. By 1977 he'd incorporated the standard modifications (see Chapter 12), with special attention to cockpit rigidity. He also added a new trick: welding in a tube that tied the forward lower A-arm mounts together.

Robertson believed the Seven's suspension showed its age in the lack of compliance and use of rubber bushings. He discarded all of the rubber and used nylon or delrin equivalents where the front A-arms and diff arm picked up the chassis. The differential pickup for the A-bracket, steering ball-joints and rear radius arms were fitted with spherical rod end bearings (rose joints). Robertson felt that many of the earlier front chassis failures were caused by heavy binding in the suspension, especially at the bracket that holds the top arm. The arm was normally located through a rubber bushing, but the sway bar loaded the rubber so heavily that the arm would bind even in steady state. Again, the fix was the substitution of a spherical bearing for the rubber bush.

The new generation of tires aided front end stickability to a significant degree and understeer became less of a problem. Robertson capitalized on the car's light weight by using Goodyear Formula Ford tires. Apparently the Goodyears were more highly developed than the tires for production cars, but the other class-D machines were too heavy to use them. With the advantage of excellent adhesion, Robertson began to balance the suspension system. A rear anti-roll bar was mounted in the luggage area, picking up the rear axle by vertical rods. Robertson chose comparatively soft springs at 140 pounds per inch at the front and 100 pounds per inch at the rear, with Spax adjustable shocks also at soft settings. With the combination of Formula car tires, minimal roll resistance and adjustable sway bars (by changing diameter), he could fine tune his Seven to just the amount of oversteer preferred.

Brakes were standard except for braided stainless steel lines and soft compound pads and shoes. Robertson solved the rear axle problem by using, ironically, TR 7 items machined to fit. A new Spitfire differential

When Sevens Take To The Air . . .

". . . Damn! Just when I was getting the feel of the course."

An original Lotus factory hoop. This driver is very brave.
Photo: Dennis Ortenburger

An original factory hoop with some additions. This driver has
friend who's learning how to weld. *Photo: Dennis Ortenburge*

Full width plus two braces. *Photo: Dennis Ortenburger*

Full width plus two braces, two diagonals and gussets.

A single diagonal plus two backstays.
Photo: Dennis Ortenburger

. . . Similar to above with padding to help prevent damage to the asphalt. *Photo: Dennis Ortenburger*

. . . Rounded corners for smoother rollovers.
Photo: Dennis Ortenburger

. . . For three point landings. *Photo: Dennis Ortenburger*

144

Show . . . and Go. Jim and Judy
Gallaghers' championship slalom
Seven in street garb and in gum-
balls *Photos: Jake Grubb; Dennis
Ortenburger*

nose piece resulted in his only protest. At Road Atlanta in 1977, British
Leyland protested the Spitfire case on the grounds that Lotus had never
used them. The chief steward ruled the case was only a bearing carrier
and the rules allowed free choice, so the protest was disallowed. That
was the year Robertson beat the TR 7's and took the Championship.

The SCCA had finally accepted the 116E Ford engine and Robertson
used the power plant bored 40 over. A dry sump, single Weber and a
free flow and tuned exhaust manifold were the significant visuals. Inside were some tricks best left unpublished, but the engine was built
more for reliability than ultimate horsepower. Typically, Robertson's
116E gave a season's racing on the same set of bearings, valves and the
like.

Tom Robertson signed to drive for Porsche in the 1980 season, but
fills his spare time building replicas of his championship car. In 1979
the SCCA Championships at Road Atlanta saw the TR 7's first victory,
but second was Pete Lobianco in a Lotus Super Seven.

Slaloming With The Gallaghers

Slaloming, or autocrossing, in the U.S. has been described as road racing on a postage stamp. In this country the sport may be the ideal outlet for a Seven owner's racing aspirations. Circuits are laid out on disused airfields, large parking lots, race tracks or any place where there is room to design a course with a running time of about one minute. Rubber pylons line the course. If any is displaced, the driver is assessed a time penalty. Cars run singly against an electronic timing apparatus measuring to a hundredth or, in some cases, a thousandth of a second. While competition is generally low-key, various organizing bodies, including the SCCA, have set up classes with season points standings, and the racing can get very serious. There are classes for stock, prepared (minimal tire, engine and suspension changes), modified (anything goes) and specials—a group for every budget and level of skill.

The Lotus Seven lends itself ideally to slaloming, due to its small dimensions, excellent handling, smart acceleration and outward visibility. An excellent model for the potential slalomer is Jim Gallagher, who has campaigned a Series 3 Lotus Seven since he purchased the car from Norwich in 1968.

Jim and Judy Gallagher take slaloming very seriously, in a relaxed sort of way. Jim Gallagher has spent years modifying and remodifying his Gallagher 7, all the while competing and looking for more performance. Not one to accept advice on faith alone, he built 2-foot chassis models out of welding rod to perform stress and deformation tests. The chassis has been strengthened by the usual methods (see Chapter 12). Additional bracing, not as uncomfortable as it looks, has been placed inside the cockpit footwells to eliminate mid-chassis bending.

Gallagher modified the suspension based on his experience in earlier seasons. The car was lowered by using shorter springs. Their rates were increased as well. Gallagher added a rear sway bar and heavier front bar; fitted the car with 10-inch-wide alloy wheels and road racing slicks. But the real fun began with the engines.

In 1969 and 1970 the Gallagher 7 ran the stock 116E crossflow. Jim won almost every event and took numerous TTD's, a credit to both driver and car. At the time, slalom classes were based on displacement so the Seven had a distinct advantage going in. A Lotus twin-cam was installed in 1971 and performance-modified in 1972. Gallagher continued to win almost every event, but a championship eluded him. By then the new Mazda rotary engine had caught his eye. Power, torque, and absolute smoothness were obvious advantages, but the change would place the car in the modified class, where specials based on Formula car chassis were beating everything in sight.

Gallagher decided to go for it and in went a Mazda RX2. Both Gallaghers took class championships. Zero to sixty times were down to 4.5 seconds, but Jim thought the car could be quicker still. The change to an alloy flywheel in 1974 made the Gallagher 7 invincible. The Gallaghers were undefeated in the Southern California Championship Slalom Series that year. Realizing the pitfalls of tampering with a proven winner, Jim nonetheless installed the larger displacement RX4 engine in 1975. Constant experimentation with carburetors resulted in a bad year. A Weber 48 IDA was fitted in 1976 and Jim took another Championship; ditto in 1978. In 1980, Jim and Judy took dual championships again.

MODIFYING THE SERIES 4

Southern California slalom racer Paul Horkin believed in the Series 4 from the beginning, despite the cult. Various handling problems arose during his several seasons of competition, so he and Jim Gallagher experimented with frame models to try and duplicate what was taking

Jim Gallagher holds scale model of space frame he built to study stress effects.

RX4 rotary has single Weber 48 IDA carburetor.

place on the race course. Their experience on the track and with the wire miniatures showed the rear of the chassis to be the prime offender, with a little cowl flex thrown in as well. Unfortunately, the main fiberglass tub had to be removed to add the necessary tubes for correction. With thousandths of a second at stake, the results were well worth the trouble.

The first modification was at the extreme rear of the chassis, at the points where the suspension arms attach. Flexing at these places allowed both unwanted suspension movement and contact with the fiberglass bodywork, which ultimately broke up from the pounding. The fix was simple enough and consisted of placing a tube inside the luggage compartment to link the two ends of the suspension arms and chassis. Threaded inserts at the ends of the tube took the place of the nuts that originally held the arms to the chassis.

There were indications that the rear suspension bay forward of the axle was lozenging. To effect a cure, Horkin welded new diagonals from the lower cross member to the chassis tower below the gas tank. Additional forward-facing diagonals were added to the same crossmember to

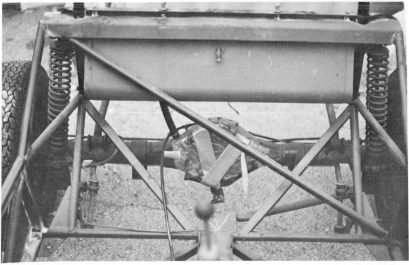

To stop unwanted suspension movement in his Series 4, Horkin placed tube across chassis back to connect two suspension arms and chassis. Threaded inserts in tube accept mounting bolts. A rear sway bar (barely visible) hugs the axle and diff housing and helps make for a more neutral-steering Series 4, according to Tom Robertson. To strengthen the rear, Horkin welded upward diagonals from center of lower member to each chassis corner, as shown in bottom photo.
Photos: Dennis Ortenburger

triangulate the under-seat area. Gallagher favored strengthening the scuttle by adding footwell braces a la the Rotary 7, but Horkin decided to live with the flex in that area until a more comfortable alternative could be designed.

The rear anti-roll bar was another Gallagher modification. A Cadillac front bar (0.70 inches in diameter) was shortened and bent to follow the differential contour. Tom Robertson also believes a rear sway bar is mandatory for a neutral-steering Series 4. His installation requires mounting the bar in the trunk area with long vertical links through the bodywork to pick up the suspension. This installation also requires trading the gas tank for a Series 2 item mounted on the floor of the luggage space.

There is obviously still more to slalom preparation, including tires, LSD's, adjustable anti-roll bars and the like. Rather than fuel any more fires, this section will simply conclude with an adage from the slalom racer's handbook: "To go quickly one must begin by proceeding slowly."

Vintage Racing With Tony Griffith

The revival of vintage and historic racing in England and the sudden interest in similar events in the U.S. has opened another avenue to Lotus Seven motorsport. In America, the sport is still in infancy and confusion reigns. Some organizers allow racing slicks while others don't. Some parts of the country allow only pre-1960 cars while others cut off at 1965. The spirit of most rules is that the cars race in their original form. Yet state-of-the-art engine, suspension and chassis modifications are allowed. The advice here is to investigate your local club's rules before preparing or purchasing a Seven, to make sure car and equipment are eligible. Whatever the club rules, Lotus Sevens are appearing in various locales with numbers on their doors . . . chassis sides, that is . . . and ready to race. That is the point of vintage racing really: to enjoy these cars at the speed and in the place they were meant to be.

When Tony Griffith came to Southern California from England, he brought with him a very interesting Series 2 Seven. Originally raced in English modsports, the car had been more or less converted to street trim. None of the Seven's speed or excellence in detailing was lost in the process.

Tony Griffith. *Photo: Dennis Ortenburger*

Molded-in instrument binnacle serves as wind deflector, too.

The engine is a Cosworth 116E, although the revs sound more like an overhead cam. Front suspension is by double wishbones with a separate, adjustable anti-roll bar. A neat trick is fenders that closely hug the tires and turn with the wheels. Reminiscent of the 7½ (page 114) with long parallel links outside the body, the rear suspension is mainly Lotus 41—complete with rubber donuts. A square tube subframe was added to support the Lotus Elite differential and to locate the lower wishbone and top arm. All link-ups are by spherical bearings, including the adjustable rear sway bar. Brakes are discs mounted out-board all around. The body is interesting also in that the scuttle has been lowered and a molded-in instrument binnacle serves as a wind deflector. The usual chassis stiffeners were added, as was a substantial roll-over bar.

All very nice to look at, but how does it go? Incredibly fast. Griffith so out-distances his own class in historic events, he finds himself grouped with larger and faster cars. It's no fun running by yourself anyway. Nonetheless, at the Times Grand Prix Historic races at Riverside, California, in April 1980, he was somewhat surprised to see himself gridded with the 1957-1965 GT cars. The Seven would be racing against a pair of Ferrari 250 GT's, a pair of Aston Martin DB4's, a Porsche Carerra, an Abarth Carerra, two Corvettes, an Alfa GTZ, a Lotus Elan, an Abarth 1300 and a host of others.

At flag fall Griffith was in the middle of the field. An Aston Martin and a Ferrari broke to the front and began pulling what looked like an insurmountable lead. Griffith masterfully reeled in the cars placed third and fourth, but surely Riverside's high speeds would hold him there to the finish. Not so! The margin to the leaders was disappearing with each lap. By the sixth circuit the Aston was passed and the tiny Seven was nipping at the heels of the Ferrari. The next lap saw Griffith take an impossible line through Turn Nine which allowed him to get inside the Ferrari and pull away. The Ferrari spun trying to catch up and Griffith won with a staggering 19-second interval over second place. Not bad for a 1½-liter push rod!

Griffith Seven employs double wishbone front suspension with separate adjustable sway bar. Fender is mounted to wheel hub and turns with tire. At the back, a square tube subframe permits use of Lotus Elite diff for independent rear suspension. Subframe also locates lower wishbone and top arm.
Photos: Dennis Ortenburger

12

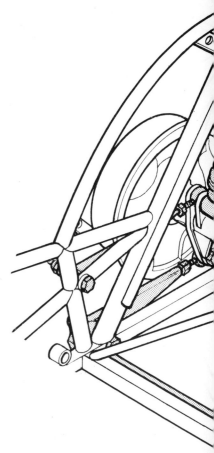

Ultimate rear suspension modification as developed by DSK Cars is shown. This system uses four adjustable trailing arms with rod ends for compliance. Note the shorter torque path. The lower trailing arms are modified with square sockets to accept a quick-change sway bar, which can be removed and re-installed without jacking the car or pulling a wheel. Lateral location is by Panhard rod, secured between chassis and a tower welded to the axle case. Tray behind axle accommodates fuel cell and enclosed battery box. Shock absorber bottoms are fitted with spherical bearings to reduce binding in roll. *Drawing: Paul Wasserboehr*

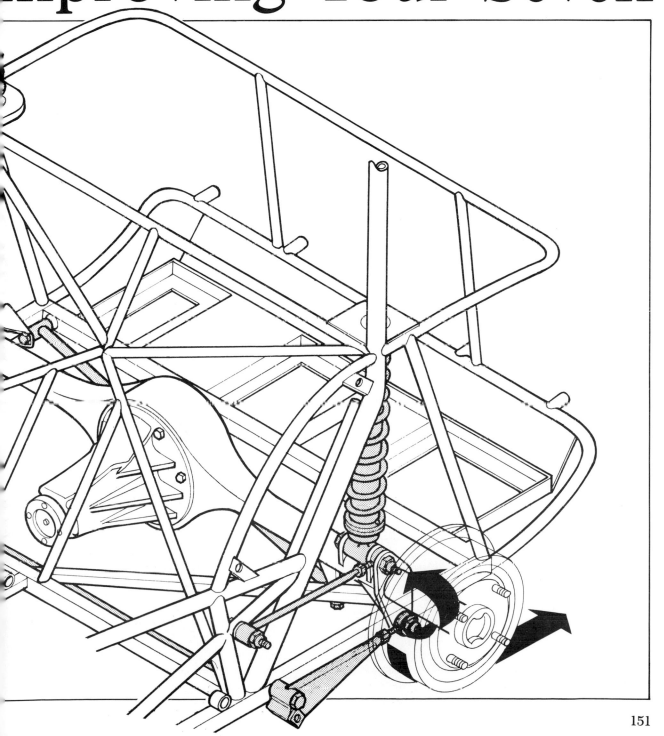

The cost of a new Caterham or Netherlands Seven has climbed well beyond Chapman's original concept. Even so, in light of the money required to buy any automobile these days, a new Seven is a relative bargain. Still sold as kits, each car is hand-assembled by enthusiastic individuals with more than a little at stake in how well they do the job. In contrast, today's replicar phenomenon has escalated the price of nostalgia well beyond the realm of reason—and most buyers are purchasing fantasy. When you acquire a Seven, at least you get the real thing.

The foregoing comments are not simply academic. The value of a used or even ancient Lotus Seven has risen to the point where restoration and careful maintenance are about as good a hedge against inflation as any you might find. And to quote Lotus guru Doug Nye, "A good running and solid Seven can give an enthusiast his second-greatest pleasure."

Fortunately, the Seven's mysteries and miseries have been unraveled, and cures exist for most all the old mechanical and structural problems. These cures are outlined in this chapter, and the names and addresses of those involved with keeping the cars alive and well are listed in Appendix 1. In America, however, two companies in particular are synonymous with the Seven: Dave Bean Engineering in Santa Barbara, California, and DSK Cars Inc. in Marblehead, Massachusetts. Both deserve more than just a mention.

Dave Bean Engineering

Dave Bean discovered the Lotus Seven mystique by racing one. His first car was purchased in 1967 and the next two seasons taught him an expensive variation of Murphy's Law—whatever could break eventually did. Axles, diffs, chassis tubes, oil coolers, radiators, wheels and bushings all at one time or another bit the dust. Bean even crashed his car twice; once on a freeway offramp while sorting understeer and once on the Riverside racetrack when a TR pushed him into the wall at Turn One. Murphy was particularly busy that day—another racer slammed into the tow truck as it was hauling Bean's Seven away.

Most men would have packed it in as a bad idea, but most men don't race Lotus Sevens. Bean recalls, "It was just too fast a car to give up on." So in 1971 he bought a new chassis and incorporated the modifications he'd learned in the previous seasons. He qualified for the National Runoffs in 1972, but insurmountable engine problems scuttled his chances for a win. At that point, Bean decided to sell his racer to bankroll his growing Lotus Seven engineering business. He had gained a justified reputation for knowing the Seven inside and out, and became a focal point for advice on race preparation, engine tuning, and the like.

One of the first items Bean devised for sale was a "swinging" oil pickup for the Ford engine. Even though most Seven racers used a gated sump, sufficient cornering loads could be attained to sweep the oil away from the pickup to the everlasting detriment of the bearings. Next Bean decided the Standard 10 axle had caused enough problems, and he began manufacturing his own copy to a stronger specification, eventually supplying even Caterham with them. When Cosworth stopped making performance parts for the Ford engines (1975), he began manufacturing duplicates. Valves, valve gear, head modifications and dry sumps are only a part of his inventory.

Dave Bean Engineering became a Caterham agent in 1977, and he can supply complete Seven kits to U.S. enthusiasts. Chassis rebuilds and modifications for older Sevens are also undertaken, as are rebuilds for engine and suspension. One suspension modification Bean particularly favors is converting the front to a double wishbone with separate anti-roll bar. He believes bump steer, front and rear, is the car's worst enemy and

Dave Bean.

152

has worked out several modifications to lessen the effect.

Even though his company has now broadened its scope to include service and parts for all Lotus cars, past and present, Bean continues to view the Seven as pure fun. Especially when he has the chance to drop in a BDA 2-liter and "go hunting for Turbo Porsches."

David S. Kaplan of DSK.
Photo: DSK Cars Inc.

DSK Cars Inc.

David S. Kaplan's first Seven was a 1964 Series 2, paid for by assembling Seven kits for Import Plaza Lotus Dealers in Massachusetts. His lasting impression of that Seven was "winding down the Mohawk Trail through the Berkshires, heat on full trickle, right foot buried in the twin SU's. It was Nürburgring in a Formula 1 car for me." The memory lingered, even as he ran an advertising business for Autodynamics, a well-known Formula car manufacturer of the late sixties located in Marblehead, Massachusetts. When Autodynamics closed doors in 1974, many of the former employees re-grouped and struck out on their own in various kinds of race car maintenance and fabrication. Kaplan did advertising for them all, as well as running a mail order formula car parts business called RaceWare Inc. In 1975 he decided to stock and sell Seven spares, with good response. Clayton Seitz came in as a partner to help go after a market they estimated at the time to be about 3000 Seven owners. Then in 1977 they approached Caterham and were appointed agents. In 1978 Kaplan & Seitz formed DSK Cars Inc., devoted exclusively to the Seven.

Seven heaven in Marblehead, Massachusetts: inside the DSK works. *Photo: DSK Cars Inc.*

153

Currently DSK handles Caterham Seven kits, restorations, the sale of previously-owned Sevens, and all manner of maintenance and service. They have developed a line of chassis and suspension modifications and publish technical bulletins to detail them. One of their specialties is the elimination of binding and frictional damping caused by the rubber bushes in the suspension. Their modification kits have been race tested and carefully developed. DSK also offers a special service for the prospective Seven buyer including a check list of what to look for and be wary of.

Kaplan and Seitz's most ambitious project to date has been the design and construction of the DSK Turbo Seven, which is covered in detail in Chapter 9.

Body Restoration—Non-Structural

Other than damage from impact or sustained local stress, the Lotus Seven body in all its guises is very reliable and durable. With the adoption of fiberglass fenders late in Series 1 production the Seven acquired a medium the amateur could repair or alter with professional results.

The most common damage to fiberglass is stress cracks, which occur when an area is hit or subject to prolonged flexing beyond its original contour. Front fenders often exhibit this kind of damage around the bolt heads holding the fender to the outriggers. Long term vibration or over-zealous bolt tightening will also lead to stress cracking. The fix is easy enough: surface-grind the offending area, resin in new cloth and finish-sand. A good preventive measure is to isolate the underside of the fender and its support with a strip of rubber.

Because Lotus factory fiberglass was color-impregnated during manufacture, any repaired section has to be repainted. Unfortunately the undersides of the front clam shells are visible and pick up stone chips very quickly. On cars where appearance is important, instead of constant re-painting, either a tinted gel coat or colored rubber sheet, such as used on the underside of alloy fenders, can be applied. The leading edges of the rear fenders take a beating from road debris as well. Here the easiest cure is to apply an alloy cover or shield as used by Caterham.

Fortunately, all of the fiberglass pieces used on the Seven are easily removable for inspection and repair. Except for the Series 4, none of the pieces are structural, so aesthetics determines how quick or dirty a repair is done.

The nose cowling on the Series 1, front cycle fenders and all bonnet covers, except again the Series 4, are alloy and present few problems. Dents can be hammered out by competent metal shops, but care should be exercised to prevent work-hardening the damaged area, which will lead later on to cracking from vibration. The Seven used thin gauge material and, like a glass panel, alloy will distort at the attachment points if careful nut tightening isn't adhered to. Vibration can lead to cracking at these points, the same as with fiberglass, and the repair technique here involves welding and metal finishing which is best left to the skilled professional.

Body Restoration—Structural

All Sevens use sheet metal which serves a dual purpose as both body covering and structural panels. The Series 4 used steel and is covered later on, but the classic Seven used alloy for the cockpit undertray, chassis sides and rear body panel. These are most important, in some places critical, because they contribute to the integrity of the chassis. Remember, the Lotus Seven is a "semi-monocoque." Inspection should be regular and repairs conducted quickly to avoid a domino effect

Rear fenders take a beating from stone chips. *Photo: John Lamm*

which weakens other areas dependent on the whole for support.

In general, the critical areas on any Seven's alloy panels are those places which take on curves and those which accept point loads through brackets, bolts or rivets. The fact these stressed panels are riveted to the chassis isn't a nightmare because only a few places are failure-prone. Typically, they are near the ends of the car heavily loaded by suspension pick-ups. One area in particular is the extreme lower corner of the right rear chassis side panel. This will distort, tear, loosen rivets and otherwise wreak havoc if the inside chassis tubes have broken. The repair entails removing the panel, welding the tubes and replacing with a fresh alloy sheet.

Sounds Like Overkill But . . .

Seat belts were first installed with the Series 3, but any Seven with mounts protruding through the undertray should be examined. Ideally, belts should only be attached to frame tubes, and if a Seven doesn't have them on the driveshaft side they can be added for that purpose. A method often seen is to run a strap, ⅛-inch thick by 2-inches wide, underneath the floor from the inside to the outer seatbelt pickup. Another method, used by Caterham, consists of a sheet metal hoop inside the rear drive shaft tunnel. The hoop is riveted to the tunnel and seat belt mounts are welded to the hoop. Still another technique is to weld a tube parallel to the rear axle at the back of the cockpit. The undertray is riveted to the tube and a belt mount added to the innermost end. If all this sounds like overkill consider that a belt mount that pulls through the alloy sheet won't do much damage to the car, but will certainly lead to some for the driver!

Three different views show tranny mount inside and out. "Doubler plates" riveted to sides and bottom hold cradle in position more securely. Note substitution of bolts for rivets at bottom. *Photos: Dennis Ortenburger*

155

All of the classic Sevens use a transmission mount consisting of sheet steel formed into a cradle riveted to the inside of the driveshaft tunnel and isolated by a rubber pad. In long-term use this cradle loosens, because the rivets stretch, leaving the tranny to vibrate and generally move around. One common fix is to drill out the rivets and add doubler plates to the bottom and sides of the tunnel. However, ¼-inch bolts can be substituted for the rivets with good success, as long as the alloy has not buckled and the original holes are not ovaled.

DSK has worked out another modification replacing the steel cradle entirely. Two new tubes pick up the base of the chassis members which locate the front of the tunnel. They run parallel to the tunnel and are welded to the cross member that locates the front of the seats. A third tube is welded in to join the new pair and drilled to accept the rubber isolation pad. The three new tubes are then riveted to the undertray and tunnel. The end result is a transmission mount integrated with the chassis rather than the alloy support panels.

The Series 4 uses steel panels at the chassis sides which are welded in place. In practice they have proven quite strong and reliable, but intelligent maintenance will always include regular inspection because, unlike the alloy panels on classic Sevens, these can rust.

The fiberglass cockpit tub on the Series 4 is a stressed member, bolted to the chassis by means of threaded bobbins laminated into the glass itself. Unusual stressing or imprudent torque on the fasteners will loosen or break the bobbins free, causing at the least a new source for rattles and at the worst a weakened chassis link. One should also take into account that because of manufacturing tolerances the main body sections never fit precisely, and the distance between chassis and fiberglass is taken up by spacers or slotted holes. However, any panel that can be seen to distort on bolting up is begging failure.

Chassis Restoration

Before getting into chassis problem areas and the recommended modifications for repair or prevention, a word of reassurance and caution is necessary. While it is true that most Sevens exhibit one or more of the problems to be discussed, not all do. However, it is only prudent to be aware of potential trouble. In addition, there is always some controversy attached to modifying a space frame. The nature of a load path may be such that a failure in one location is caused by a weakness in a remote part of the frame. While most experts agree the Seven has a very flexible cockpit area, only some believe front suspension bay failures can be traced to this cockpit bending. Others feel that each section is more or less independent of the whole and should, therefore, be analyzed and modified by itself. What follows then is a consensus of generally-held opinion, except of course by the purists, who denounce any change from the original.

All Lotus Sevens, including the Series 4, had frames or chassis constructed of mild steel. Inspection would seem relatively easy, with broken or bent tubes quickly identified. Unfortunately, the worst enemy of a tube chassis is unseen: internal rust. The only effective tests are destructive and even the so-called "California cars" aren't exempt because Lotus stored their chassis outside in the mist and rain of England. About the only thing that can be done is to find all the drain/welding-vent holes and make sure they are clear.

Low Budget Fallout

There are several areas on the classic Sevens prone to frame breakage. They stem from the chassis's inherent lack of rigidity, an unfortunate result of originally designing to a tight budget, i.e. the fewer the tubes the lower the cost. The good news is that potential failures are known and can be prevented.

The most common failure is in the front suspension bay. As mentioned in earlier chapters, the intersection of vertical and horizontal tubes that carry the rearward lower A-arm pickup is the prime offender. The right-hand side seems to break more frequently than the left, but that may be related to the one original diagonal that triangulates and strengthens the

Additional triangulation or gusseted corners is required to strengthen front suspension bay, as shown top left and right.

New diagonal between vertical tube which takes rear radius arm bracket and lower chassis member supports tube properly. *Photos: Dennis Ortenburger*

left side. The fix is to triangulate each plane in the suspension bay with new diagonals and, as an additional precaution, to gusset the corners. The nose cowling, radiator and front suspension have to be removed to do acceptable welds, but this is not difficult.

Moving to another trouble-spot, pre-Caterham Lotus Sevens have the rear radius arm pickup in the middle of an unsupported vertical tube. A simple and direct modification is to weld a diagonal between the vertical tube which takes the radius arm bracket and the lower chassis member. Caterham provided the new tube on all of their Series 3's. Another troublesome point in the rear chassis is at the five-tube intersection on the lower chassis ahead of the wheel. Again, right-hand failures are more common than left, but the fix seems to be webbing the junction with corner gussets. It's generally agreed that the breakage here is caused by chassis flex in the cockpit and engine bays, because taken as a whole, the rear frame appears well supported.

The problem of flexing in the middle region of the Seven's frame has been corrected by Caterham, Donkervoort and others, but the owners of earlier cars can do the same. Adding the diamond-shaped diagonal below the engine and triangulating the top and sides of the scuttle bays help these areas. Another pair of diagonals added to the cockpit floor and running from the bottom lateral tube out to the outer chassis rail completes the reinforcement. A completely braced cockpit bay not only offers the advantage of better crash protection, but produces a more rigid chassis and therefore a better-handling Seven.

The Series 4 has none of the breakage reputation of the earlier cars, but can use a little added rigidity for racing. (Such reinforcement for both classic Sevens and the Series 4 is covered in Chapter 11.)

Although not strictly part of the chassis, mention will be made here of the Seven's gas tank attachment, or better, "purported" gas tank attachment. Early Series 1 tanks were held in place by bungee cords. While these were totally unsafe (though "proved" in Formula 1) the metal straps subsequently used on the later series weren't much better. This is because the Lotus gas tanks are constructed out of the lightest gauge steel possible. It's not that rust is a particular problem; rather, the thin-walled tank chafes against the straps and suffers from vibration cracking. Location of the tank high in the chassis where it is subject to constant tossing about compounds the problem. A tank loose in its straps is simply begging for leaks. The fix is to replace the original straps with a more substantial gauge steel and isolate between tank and strap with rubber strips.

In addition, with the exception of the Series 4 and the Netherlands Seven, all Sevens have gas tanks in an extremely vulnerable rearmost position. A safety modification worth considering is a substantial bulkhead twixt tank and rear body panel. The ultimate is, of course, a foam-filled fuel cell.

Flexing in middle of Seven space frame is corrected by triangulating top and sides of scuttle (photos upper left and right) and adding diagonal tubes below engine (photo lower left). Photos: Dennis Ortenburger

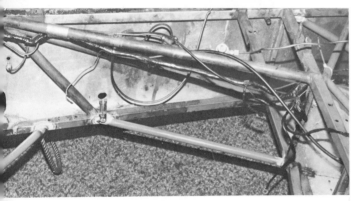

Suspension Restoration

The weakest suspension member, by far, on any early Seven is the Standard (Triumph) 10 rear axle. Ordinarily the best way around is to swap for the Escort or Cortina equivalent. Even with these, hard use can lead to leaking or a cracked banjo, but the shafts and ring and pinion are substantially longer lived. If your Seven is to be heavily stressed, it's a good idea to reinforce the banjo with buttresses. But life is not so simple. In America the SCCA won't allow the axle substitutions, so the racers are stuck with the ancient iron. And in the street, new wheels to

Gas tank should be isolated from steel retaining straps by rubber strips to prevent chafing.

suit the Escort bolt pattern have to be used, so to enjoy the luxury of the same four wheels all around, the front hubs have to be changed as well.

Buttress plate reinforcement for axle provides much needed strength to Seven's weakest link.

The axle's weaknesses are half-shafts unable to handle the torque and cornering power of modern engines/tires and an extremely flexible differential case. Modifications to the case are legion, but all employ the welding of gussets, plates or secondary support frames to eliminate bending.

Standard stopped making the Standard 10 in 1959, and by the time Lotus switched to the Escort most of the spares were long gone. To satisfy demand, replacement axles were manufactured by a number of firms. Unfortunately, some were better than others. Be sure to check the splines at the diff end and the taper at the outboard end. In search for more strength some manufacturers used wider splines based on different axles. Good idea, but a similar change has to be made to the diff gears for a proper fit. Both DSK and Dave Bean have found outboard tapers so ill-matched that torque is taken by the woodruff key, which has a predictably short life expectancy.

Another common failure also occurs in the rear suspension. On Sevens fitted with the wide-based rear A-arm, the point of the "A" is attached to the diff bottom through a rubber bushing. This rubber bush is located in an extremely vulnerable place and is attacked by oil weeping out of the differential banjo. Even under ideal conditions this bushing is highly stressed and wears rapidly. A worn bush lets the rear axle move laterally as well as up and down, making for a twitchy back-end accompanied by nasty banging noises.

Well-meaning owners have tried substituting other bushing materials, such as nylon, but in so doing the flexibility required by the original design is lost. A less compliant bushing will increase roll resistance and further stress chassis and axle. Routine inspection is one answer, with a good supply of spare bushings. One ultimate fix is a redesign, substituting a spherical bearing (rose joint) for the rubber bushing and modifying both the A-arm and diff bracket. Such a fix is available from DSK and does at least provide relief from frequent bushing replacement.

Engines

At this writing only the Ford crossflow and the Ford 2-liter as used in the Netherlands Seven are still in regular production. The immediate future holds no problems for maintenance and restoration, because spares for all the Ford variants are reasonably available worldwide. Only the 100E flathead is getting rare, but specialists still exist in England and current interest in historic car racing is helping the engine situation.

Those Series 1's which ran Climax engines are in good shape spares-wise, due to the understanding nature of Coventry Climax. Parts are still manufactured and stocked and Appendix 1 lists sources. The Lotus twin-cam has long since ceased production at Norwich, but Caterham has undertaken the old engine's entire manufacture, updating the block to the 2737E long stroke and manufacturing the head in big-valve, Weber-aspirated configuration.

The many engines used in the various Sevens each have their peculiarities, their strengths and their weaknesses. It is beyond the scope of this book to detail these characteristics, but technical assistance and information can be readily obtained through Seven specialists. The most frequent question seems to be about up-dating to a more powerful engine, and the answer is inevitably "yes"—but various brackets and fittings must first be altered. Here again is reason to seek advice from the specialists. All in all, only imagination, good sense and competent engineering are required to use just about any motor in a Seven—even a Mazda rotary.

All About A-Arms

In the black art of suspension design, Colin Chapman stands at the head of the class. His skill is reflected in the front suspension of the Seven, which is a direct lift from his Lotus 12 Formula car and also is used by the original Lotus Elite.

As previously described in Chapter 2, the Seven front is a double wishbone arrangement, using an A-frame for the lower member, but combining the anti-roll bar (sway bar) with a track rod (top link) to form the upper A-frame. Principal criticism of the design is that, while a model of simplicity and efficiency, it transmits torsional braking and cornering loads into the rubber track rod bushing and flexible sway bar. In normal road use this is of little consequence, but under racing conditions the increased stiction of slick race tires dramatically increases these forces and causes bump steer, chassis flexing and ride harshness as the sway bar pulls the top link back and forth and twists the wheel spindle forward. In addition to these problems, the original design also allows no provision for adjustment to caster, camber or roll stiffness.

The idea behind the variations shown here is to detach the anti-roll bar from the top link while still providing an upper wishbone. This is of course exactly what Chapman did when he designed the Lotus 20 Formula Junior race car, and is the suspension found on the Lotus 7½ (see Chapter 9 for a more

Lotus 12 front suspension.

complete description of this special). As shown in the photo, the sway bar is mounted above the wishbone at a new pivot point, and the sway bar is tied to the lower a-arm with an adjustable link.

DSK takes a similar approach for their Turbo Seven, but uses an adapter to accommodate both the pickup of the new upper wishbone and the sway bar pivot. The sway bar is placed slightly below the original mounting point and connects to a new triangulated lower A-frame by means of an adjustable link. The upper wishbone is attached with a ball joint permitting camber adjustment.

One of the most interesting solutions is provided by Dave Bean of Dave Bean Engineering. He retains the original top link, adds a chassis-strengthening cross member and stays SCCA legal, as no new holes are cut in the body for suspension members. First Bean removes the sway bar and bolts in its place a U-shaped cross member. This reduces flexure of the front bulkhead and uprights, and provides a heim joint (rose joint) attachment point for a trailing link which forms an upper A-arm in conjunction with the top link. The other end of the trailing link is secured by a clevis bolt at what was previously the sway bar attachment point on the top link. The last item in Bean's modification kit is a new tubular sway bar with a link to the lower A-frame similar to DSK. The one-inch tubular sway bar is fitted inside the U-channel cross member, and extends out around the newly constituted upper A-frame in a constant radius bend. In addition to modest roll rate adjustment via the link to the lower A-frame, major adjustments can be made by using a sway bar tube of different wall thickness. Bean's kit is applicable to all classic Sevens and costs about $350.

Dave Bean Engineering adds trailing link to existing track rod to form upper A-frame. New tubular sway bar fits inside new U-channel cross member.

Chapman's double wishbone arrangement as found on the Lotus 7½. *Photo: Dennis Ortenburger.*

DSK Turbo Seven front suspension uses new upper and lower A-frames, employs adapter to accommodate both sway bar pivot and pickup point for upper wishbone. *Photo: David S. Kaplan.*

Epilogue: An Inspiration For Misfits

In July 1970, Mr. William Boddy, the esteemed editor of *Motor Sport* magazine, arrived at the Lotus works in Norwich to road test a Series 4 Seven. His plan was to put the car through its paces en route to his country house in Wales some 258 miles away. Since a biting wind was blowing across the Wymondham Plains, Chapman's junior executives, under strict orders to minister to the needs of the venerable Mr. Boddy, solicitously offered to put up the folding top.

"No thank you," said Boddy, "the whole point of a Lotus Seven is to enjoy lots of fresh air." He levered himself into position (nobody "jumps into" a Seven) and was off, only to find his path blocked by security guards at the main gate. Typically, no-one had thought to give him a clearance chit.

Boddy got 80 miles to St. Neots before giving in to reality and putting up the sidescreens. Frozen earlobes, however, were only the beginning of his troubles, as subsequently the clutch gave out.

"Although I can usually cope with a clutchless car . . . on this occasion it became quite impossible to engage a gear . . . ," Boddy later explained, and an unhappy Colin Chapman was forced to send a transporter to retrieve the recalcitrant Seven all the way back from Wales. Such an experience might dampen any test driver's enthusiasm for his subject, particularly one so jaded, but Boddy wasn't bothered a bit. "This Cortina GT-engined Seven was great fun," he reported in measured understatement, "and did its indicated 100 miles per hour along quite short straights."

Boddy's reaction is typical of the irrational fondness inspired by the legendary Lotus Seven. The car is unlovely to look at, uncomfortable to drive and idiosyncratic, at best. Still, people will go out and buy the car—new, used, in pieces, half dead or any other way they can find it. As a result, an automobile that should have quietly faded away in the late 60's has survived parental neglect, repudiation and even the humiliation of being recast in plastic and sent out to compete with the dune buggies. The fact that the Seven is about to celebrate its twenty-fifth year in production is inspiration for misfits everywhere.

How to account for this remarkable staying power? Price, for one thing. Chapman was able to move people where it mattered most: in the pocketbook. The kit-car approach made the Seven far less expensive than most equivalent sports cars on the road. Performance was there, too. Chapman did his number on the drawing board and came up with a power-to-weight formula that made the car truly competitive (no matter that the space frame needed a little shoring up here and there).

The price/performance combination made the Seven an attractive option. In the crowded 60's market, for example, you could buy a Basic Seven kit with Ford 105E engine in the U.K. for an irresistible 499 pounds sterling ($1400). American buyers had to pay $2900 for the Seven America with BMC engine, but the car was cheap compared to a Corvette ($3872) or Jag XKE ($5595). The MGA 1600 was lower-priced at $2485, and a real car—you could even drive it in the rain—but basically boring with 40,000 clones on the loose. A Lotus Seven bought you a lot of attention for that extra $400.

By 1962, the Super Seven version of the Series 2 debuted. The Cosworth-
tuned 109E could sprint 0-60 in a very respectable 9.9 seconds, its curb weight of
1064 pounds giving the car a clear edge over the 2080-pound MGB
(12.5 seconds), 2240-pound TR-4 (10.5 seconds) or 2430-pound Austin-Healey
3000 (11.2 seconds). The most impressive feature of this somehow street-legal car
was the price: 599 pounds ($1700) in the U.K. and $3400 in the U.S. When the
Super Seven 1500 roared into view with 0-60 times under seven seconds and a
U.K. price tag of $1800, enthusiasts could only gasp in delight.

So there was price and there is performance, but the Seven has something
else still. Low to the ground and satisfyingly noisy, it comes as close to fulfilling
the sports car fantasy as any vehicle before or since. Driving the Seven is The
Real Thing:

> The thick-rimmed steering wheel sat perfectly at arm's length and the tiny
> gear lever snuggled into my palm . . . From a standstill it's simple to drag
> away with spinning wheels and the engine pulling hard from around 3000
> rpm . . . you just blink to snatch 2nd, blink again for 3rd then top with the
> tires chirping with wheelspin in each intermediate cog! Sitting with the
> back axle fighting away just behind one's lumbar region, there's a lot of car
> up front . . . Roadholding is incredible. There's a deal of self-steering over
> ripples but the Seven runs true if you hold the wheel loosely and slinging
> through the curves and corners is just a matter of lifting one fist or the other
> an inch or two . . . It's crude, it's uncompromising, but it's also sheer,
> unadulterated, unbelievable fun.

> —Doug Nye, reporting on a ride in a Caterham
> Seven for *Road & Track*, February 1977

"Sheer, unadulterated, unbelievable fun . . ." When you're explaining the
phenomenon of the Lotus Seven, what else really needs to be said?

APPENDIX 1: COMPARISON GUIDE

But First, Some Obfuscation About Chassis Numbers . . .

It's not possible to reconstruct a chassis chronology for the Lotus Seven, for two reasons. First, the "lads in the back room" were more interested in building cars than in keeping records, and the whole operation was casual in the extreme. Then, many of the records that were kept "disappeared" when Lotus Components was dissolved in 1970. The rather sketchy production records that have surfaced are maintained by the Historic Lotus Register (see Appendix 3) and exist only for the Series 1 and for Series 2 through 1965. These records suggest the following:

Series 1 chassis numbers (11/57 to 7/60): 400 to 499 *and* 750 to 892

Series 2 chassis numbers (7/60 to 12/65): 1004 to 2101

The gap of 250 numbers in the Series 1 sequence will probably never be explained. Best guess is that the numbers were allocated to another car Lotus was building concurrently, such as the Mark 15 or 17, and not to Lotus Sevens. Lotus did build in batches, so this is a plausible, if not convenient explanation for Seven historians. The gap occurred during the summer of 1959, the 400-series apparently ending in June or July (several undated chassis numbers muddy the record at this point) and the 750-series commencing in October. This was a confused period for Lotus because of the move to Cheshunt and subsequent reorganization, which was accomplished in June of that year with an official October opening. It's quite reasonable to assume that, except for finishing a few promised cars, Lotus suspended production of the Seven for a few months while they got organized, and decided to jump to a new number sequence when operations resumed.

Additional information about chassis numbers appears in the Seven *Owner's Manual*, but some of it seems dubious. The date of commencement of manufacture of Series 1 cars, for example, is given as February 1958, which is clearly not true (at least eight were produced in late 1957).

According to the manual, Series 2 cars, including American and Super Seven models, carry the prefix "SB" on chassis number plates beginning with SB 1000 (in other words, all Series 2's). The prefix doesn't show up in the records, however, until SB 1381. The manual goes on to say that LHD vehicles were assigned special blocks of numbers, namely SB 1500 – 1550 and SB 1750 – 1799. This seems questionable, too. While a few of the records for cars in these ranges are marked LHD, there's nothing to indicate if the others were LHD or not. Records also indicate that cars 1083 to 1119 were shipped to Jay Chamberlain who was the sole distributor in the U.S., and surely at least some of these would have been LHD.

The *Owner's Manual* states that cars produced after October 1963 added the prefix "L" to indicate LHD, and this indeed appears to be the case in the records beginning with LSB 2014 in May 1965. After the numbers 1500 – 1550 and 1750 – 1799 were used up, LHD and RHD cars shared the same number ranges, with the added "L" being the only differentiation.

The total number of cars produced in each series can only be estimated now, based on existing records and educated guesses. Best guesses are Series 1, 242 cars; Series 2, 1350 cars; Series 3, 350 cars and Series 4, 1000 cars. This brings the total number of Sevens produced to 2942, which is 358 shy of Chapman's "official" figure of 3300. It's a puzzle, all right.

	SERIES 1	SERIES 2
PRODUCTION:	1957 to 1960. Approximately 242 cars built.	1960 to 1968. Approximately 1350 cars built.
CHASSIS:	Multi-tube space frame developed from Lotus Eleven. Stressed alloy undertray, transmission tunnel, body sides and rear form semi-monocoque.	Lightened version of Series 1 space frame, with fewer tubes.
BODY:	All alloy panels, including nose cowl, bonnet, scuttle, rear panel, front cycle fenders and separate rear fenders. Slight downward slope to nose cowl; "egg crate" grille. Headlights, fender-mounted side lamps, twin stop lights. Full-width windscreen. Optional fabric top and tonneau cover. FIA fabric doors available late in production.	Alloy cycle fenders initially fitted on English models; with fiberglass "clam shells" on Seven America. Clam shells later fitted on all models. Fiberglass rear fenders. Fiberglass cowling squared off and continuous with hood line. "Barbeque-screen" grille. Folding top, spare tire and windscreen wipers standard equipment. Rear quarter windows, top and hinged sidescreens available.
STEERING:	Burman worm-and-nut, updated to Elite rack-and-pinion; 2½ turns lock-to-lock. Rack positioned back of wheel. Right-hand drive only.	Triumph Herald rack, moved ahead of wheel center line; 2¾ turns lock-to-lock. Right- or left-hand drive.
BRAKES:	8″ × 1½″ drums front and rear.	Drums front and rear: 8″ × 1¼″ front; 7″ × 1¼″ rear.
WHEELS:	Lightweight bolt-on 15″ diameter on 4″ rims. Optional wire wheels.	13″ diameter on 3½″ Triumph rims. 4½″ to 5″ rims later allowed. Optional wire wheels dropped.
SUSPENSION:	Independent at front with lower wishbone and top member formed by intersection of top arm and anti-roll bar (identical with Elite). Live rear axle from Standard (Triumph) 10 located by trailing arms and diagonal member.	Same as Series 1 at front except for relocation of steering rack. At rear, diagonal tube traded for large A-bracket that picked up lower chassis near parallel locating arms and attached to differential at point.
MODELS/ENGINES:	*Seven F (Basic)* – Ford 100E 1172-cc sidevalve (flathead) engine, 40 bhp, Ford 3-speed gearbox. Spare tire optional. *Seven F (Export)* – Tuned Ford 100E with twin SU's, 4-branch exhaust, higher compression ratio, 3-speed gearbox. Tachometer and spare tire standard equipment. *Seven C (Super Seven)* – Coventry Climax FWA 1097-cc engine, 75 bhp, BMC 4-speed gearbox. Wire wheels with 4-inch rims standard. *Seven A* – BMC 948-cc engine, 37 bhp, BMC 4-speed gearbox. *Seven A America* – BMC 948-cc engine, 37 bhp, BMC 4-speed gearbox. Fiberglass fenders, clam shell style in front with turn indicators on top. Separate turn signals and stop lights mounted to rear fender backs. Fabric top, tonneau, FIA fabric doors, carpets, spare tire, tachometer and fan standard equipment.	*Seven F* – Ford 100E 1172-cc sidevalve (flathead) engine. Ford 3-speed gearbox. *Seven A* – BMC 948- or 1098-cc, 37/55 bhp, single SU/twin SU, 4-branch exhaust, Sprite 4-speed gearbox. *Seven A America* – BMC 948- or 1098-cc, 43/55 bhp, twin SU's, increased compression. Sprite 4-speed gearbox. *Basic Seven* – Ford 105E. Introduced 1961. Replaced Seven A/Seven A America ("America" designation dropped). 997-cc engine, 50 bhp, twin SU's or single Weber 40-DCOE sidedraft, 4-branch exhaust. Ford Anglia 4-speed all synchro gearbox. *Super Seven Ford 109E* – Introduced 1961. 1340-cc engine, 85 bhp, twin Webers, Cosworth head, 4-branch exhaust, Ford Classic gearbox. *SCCA Cosworth 109E* – SCCA racing version of Super Seven Ford 109E, with compression raised to 10.5 to 1. *Super Seven 1500* – Introduced 1962. Ford 116E 1498-cc Cortina engine, 66 bhp, 5-main-bearing crankshaft, single Weber 40-DCOE. Cortina GT gearbox. 9½″ diameter Girling disc brakes fitted at front. Tonneau and fabric doors standard equipment. *Cosworth Super Seven 1500* – Cosworth-tuned Ford 116E, 95 bhp, twin Webers, 4-branch exhaust, high lift cam shaft.
*KIT PRICE:	U.K.: Seven F – £587 ($1643) U.K.: Seven C – £700 ($1960) U.K.: Seven A – £611 ($1710) U.S.: Seven A America – $2897 *All kit prices include engine and gearbox, unless otherwise indicated	U.K., 1961: Kit less engine and gearbox – £399 ($1100) Basic Seven with 105E engine – £499 ($1400) U.K., 1962: Super Seven 109E – £599 ($1700) Super Seven 1500 – £585 ($1600) U.K., 1965: Basic Seven with 105E engine £499 ($1400) U.S., 1962: Super Seven 109E – $3395 Basic Seven 105E – $3190

165

COMPARISON GUIDE

	SERIES 3	SERIES 4
PRODUCTION:	1968 to 1970. Approximately 350 cars built.	1970 to 1973. Approximately 1000 cars built.
CHASSIS:	Initially identical to Series 2 except for additional pick-ups for mounting new exhaust silencer and extended tailpipe. Tubes added later to reinforce rear trailing arm chassis mount; and triangulate bottom engine bay and chassis sides.	Complete redesign to separate body on tube and ladder frame. Stressed sheet steel side panels. Slightly wider and longer than previous models.
BODY:	Detail changes only from Series 2: wider rear fenders with sharper radius, air scoop or louvers added to bonnet top, gas tank filler moved to rear body panel, new perforated muffler shroud and exhaust pipe exiting at rear, separate amber turn signals mounted beneath headlights, seat belt mounts standard. Optional roll-over bar. Redesigned dash panel with fuel gauge and rocker switches.	All fiberglass, molded in four sections. Front and rear fenders restyled and lengthened. Hinged bonnet incorporating frontal air intake and carb air scoop; battery moved from bonnet to luggage area. Side windows given sliding panels for ventilation. Rear quarter windows removed from soft top. Optional hard top with opening window. Lap belts standard equipment; roll-over bar optional. Finished-look cockpit with individual seats, column-mounted levers, redesigned dash with recessed center panel.
STEERING:	Triumph Herald rack, 2¾ turns lock-to-lock. Steering rack raised late in production to bring steering arms nearly parallel to ground. Right- or left-hand drive.	Burman rack-and-pinion, 2¾ turns lock-to-lock. Collapsible and adjustable Triumph steering column. Right- or left-hand drive.
BRAKES:	9″ discs front; 8″ × 1½″ drums rear.	8½″ discs front; 9″ drums rear. Elan "umbrella pull" handbrake.
WHEELS:	Escort steel 13″ diameter on 5½″ rims. Brand Lotus alloy rims optional.	Identical to Series 3.
SUSPENSION:	Standard (Triumph) 10 rear axle changed to wider track Ford Escort; otherwise identical to Series 2. Front wheel hubs changed to suit Escort 4¼″ bolt circle.	Double wishbone at front, with separate anti-roll bar picking up bottom of shock absorber; derived from Lotus Europa. Quadruple linkage at rear with both leading and trailing arms locating Escort axle and revised A-bracket. Optional limited slip differential.
MODELS/ ENGINES:	*Economy* – Ford 225E 1300-cc Escort GT, 68 bhp, Cortina 116E gearbox. *Standard* – Ford 2250E 1600-cc Cortina crossflow, 84 bhp, 4-branch exhaust, twin choke Weber downdraft type 32 DFM. Cortina 116E gearbox. *Super Seven Twin Cam* (Lotus Seven SS) – Lotus 1600-cc twin-cam engine, 90 bhp, or Holbay-modified to 125 bhp (twin Weber 40-DCOE's, free flow 4-branch exhaust, higher lift cams). Lucas taillights changed to rectangular 3-sectioned Britax unit incorporating stoplight, turn indicator and taillight.	Same as Series 3, but "Super Seven" nomenclature dropped. All equipped with Corsair 2000E gearbox; engine-driven fan.
* KIT PRICE:	U.K.: Standard – £775 ($1860) U.K.: Super Seven Twin-Cam – £1250 ($3000)	U.K., 1970: 1600 – £895 ($2160) Twin-cam – £995 ($2400) U.K., 1972: 1600 – 1070 ($2780) Twin-cam – £1295 ($3370)

CATERHAM SEVEN

1973 to date.

Improved Series 3 space frame with additional tubes to strengthen chassis sides, engine bay and rear suspension pick-ups.

Series 3 design with slightly raised nose piece and bonnet; rectangular Britax taillight unit incorporating stop light, taillight and turn indicator. Improved seat belt mounts and optional redesigned roll bar. Interior revised to give more space. Return to toggle switches on dash.

Rack-and-pinion, with heavier steering rack mounting blocks. Right- or left-hand drive.

Twin circuit system with 9″ discs front and 9″ drums rear.

Brand Lotus or Goodyear alloy 13″ diameter on 6″ rims.

As Series 3, but rear axle updated to Escort RS2000.

Ford 225E 1600-cc Cortina crossflow or Lotus 1600-cc twin cam, with Corsair 2000E gearbox and Kenlowe-type electric fan. Twin-cam produced by Caterham since 1980.

U.K., 1979: Twin-cam – £5000 pounds ($11,250)
U.S., 1981: 1600 – $13,600
Twin-cam – $14,950

NETHERLANDS SEVEN

1977 to date.

Redesigned Series 3 space frame with additional chassis rails under cockpit; lower engine and transmission bays. Wheelbase stretched by 2.73″. Cockpit widened by 5½″ with 3½″ more leg room. Engine and gearbox moved slightly rearward for better weight distribution.

Series 3 design with detail changes: louvered bonnet with large carb intake scoop; slightly flared rear fenders to accommodate larger wheels. Twin gas tanks fitted ahead of rear axle, resulting in expanded luggage bin. Roomier cockpit with bucket seats.

Rack-and-pinion; left-hand drive only.

Identical to Caterham Seven.

Revolution alloy 14″ diameter on 7″ rims.

Ford Escort rear axle located by leading and trailing arms plus Panhard rod, similar to Series 4. Front identical to Caterham Seven.

Type B – Ford 1600-cc crossflow engine
Type D Super Seven – Ford Escort RS2000 single overhead cam engine, 110 bhp.

1980: Type B – 22,000 guilders ($8950)
Type D – 26,000 guilders ($10,600)

RATES OF EXCHANGE

During the period covered in this volume, the exchange rate between the British pound and the U.S. dollar was relatively stable. The prices given in the text are based on the following rates of exchange:

Prices for the Netherlands Seven were calculated at the rate of 1 guilder = $0.4072.

1950 – 1967 . . . . £1 = $2.80
1968 – 1971 . . . . £1 = $2.40
1972 . . . . £1 = $2.60
1973 – 1974 . . . . £1 = $2.50
1979 . . . . £1 = $2.25

APPENDIX 2: SEVEN WEIGHTS AND MEASURES (in pounds and inches)

	SERIES 1		SERIES 2				
		BMC	105E	109E	109E Cosworth	116E	116E Cosworth
Weight[1]	897 [2]	960	952	1015	1064	1034	—
Wheelbase	88	88	88	88	88	88	88
Front track	47	48.5	47	47.5	49	—	—
Rear track	46½	48.5	47	48.5	49	—	—
Overall length	123	132	144	131.2	131¼	144	144
Overall width[3]	53	58.3	56	57.2	57½	56	56
Overall height	44	43	43	44.7	43½	43	43
Minimum ground clearance	5	6.5	6.5	5.0	4	6	6

Somehow it's not surprising, considering the Seven's somewhat irreverent nature, that consistent weight and measurement figures for the car are impossible to find. (In some cases, any figures at all are impossible to find.) Granted, measurement techniques, especially for the early models, were frequently less than scientific compared with current methodology. Afterall, the first Series 1 Seven appeared over 20 years ago. Techniques differed among testers, too. The weight of a car could vary tremendously: with fluids or without, with driver or without, with passenger or without. One tester weighed the car with "enough fuel to drive approximately 50 miles." Similarly, height and ground clearance measurements differ according to tire size and engine capacity. So far, divergences in the statistics are perfectly understandable. How does one explain, however, the phenomenon of a Seven that gains 12 or 13 inches in length between tests? Or inexplicably shrinks a couple of inches around the middle? One can't. One can only gather all available test data and present a set of figures that are as consistent as possible. Don't bother to rush out to your Seven with yardstick and scale—your version is sure to be slightly off the "norm." Whatever it measures, it's close enough. Afterall, the Lotus Seven was never meant to be taken too seriously.

[1] *Unless otherwise indicated, weight is* curb weight, *i.e., a car weighed with fluids but wit[ ] driver or passenger.*

[2] *This weight is for 7A. The 7F weighed 725 lb. Both figures are weight of car* without

[3] *According to the Owner's Manual, the clam shell fenders add two inches in width.*

[4] *Weight of 1300 and 1600. Twin-cam: 1260 lb.*

[5] *Figure available for twin-cam only.*

[6] *Twin-cam: 1310 lb.*

[7] *Twin-cam: 1125 lb.*

SERIES 3	SERIES 4	CATERHAM SEVEN	NETHERLANDS SEVEN (D-TYPE)	
Ford 225E	Ford 225E	Ford 225E	Ford 225E	
1204 ④	1200 ⑥	1106 ⑦	—	
89	90	88½	91	(2.31m)
49	48.8	50	51	(1.29m)
52	52	52	53	(1.35m)
133	146.3	133	140	(3.56m)
61	60.5	62.2	59	(1.50m)
37	44	44	37	(0.94m)
3 ⑤	6.5	4	—	

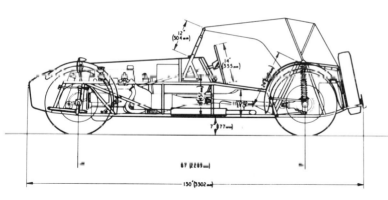

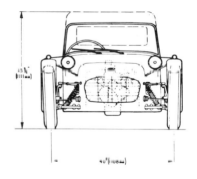

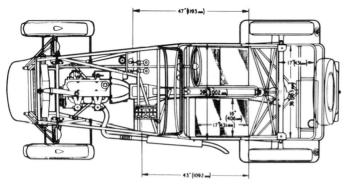

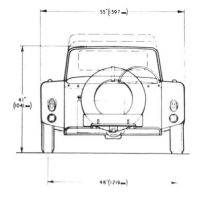

LOTUS SEVEN
SERIES TWO

MANUFACTURED AND DISTRIBUTED BY
LOTUS COMPONENTS LTD.
DELAMARE ROAD, CHESHUNT, HERTS.   Tel Waltham Cross 26181

APPENDIX 3: LOTUS SEVEN SOURCE LIST

AGENTS AND MANUFACTURERS

Caterham Car Sales
Seven House
Town End
Caterham Hill
Surrey CR3 5UG
ENGLAND

Builder: Caterham Seven, Lotus twin-cam engine. Spares for all Lotus Seven series, race prep and coachwork.

DSK Cars, Inc.
14 Pond Street
Marblehead
Massachusetts 01945
U.S.A.

Builder: Series 3 Turbo; agent for Caterham Seven kits, spares for Lotus Seven Series 1-4, race prep and restoration.

Dave Bean Engineering
925 Punta Gorda Street
P.O. Box 4070
Santa Barbara, California 93103
U.S.A.

Agent for Caterham Seven kits, spares for Lotus Seven Series 1-4, race prep, restoration and coachwork.

The Netherlands Seven
Laan Van Niftarlake 10
3612 BS Tienhoven (Utr.)
THE NETHERLANDS

Builder: Series 3 Super Seven to wide chassis D- and B-Types; spares and coachwork.

Steel Bros. (NZ) Ltd.
1-31 Treffers Road
Sockburn
Christchurch 4
NEW ZEALAND

Builder: Series 4

Dutton Cars Ltd., Unit 10
Ham Bridge Trading Estate
East Worthing, West Sussex
BN14 8NA
ENGLAND

Builder: Dutton Phaeton

Dutton Cars, Inc.
120½ Northshore Drive
Knoxville, Tennessee 37919
U.S.A.

Agent for Dutton Phaeton kits; parts and service

Coventry Climax Engines Ltd.
Coventry
ENGLAND

Manufacturer of Coventry Climax engines

Hutton Motor Engineering
P.O. Box 351
Clarksville, Tennessee 37040
U.S.A.

Supplier of Coventry Climax spares

LOTUS SEVEN CLUBS

Historic Lotus Register
Badgerswood
School Road
Drayton
Norwich NR8 6EF
ENGLAND

Club Lotus U.K.
107 Brandon Road
Watton
Norfolk
ENGLAND

Club Lotus Australia
40 Bellambi Street
Northbridge
New South Wales
AUSTRALIA

German Lotus Club
Kaiser-Friedrich Ring 33
4000 Düsseldorf 11
WEST GERMANY

Lotus Ltd.
P.O. Box L
College Park, Maryland 20740
U.S.A.

Lotus/West Inc.
P.O. Box 75972
Los Angeles, California 90005
U.S.A.